INEVITABLE

Inevitable

The Identity Shift Behind Lasting Influence and Authority

Keisha Leilani

Published by Game Changer Publishing

Paperback ISBN: 979-8-90158-301-2
Hardcover ISBN: 979-8-90158-126-1
Digital ISBN: 979-8-90158-127-8

www.GameChangerPublishing.com

INEVITABLE

The Identity Shift Behind Lasting Influence and Authority

KEISHA LEILANI

To my kids, you have been my greatest motivation, even before you were born. I wanted to become a role model you could look to when facing challenges and when learning to turn every opportunity into growth. Own who you are, don't be swayed by outside influences, and be your own North Star as you work to make a meaningful difference in the world.

ADVANCE PRAISE

"Keisha is a master connector who effortlessly brings people together, both online and in person, creating spaces where real relationships can grow. Her warmth and genuine care turn strangers into collaborators and acquaintances into lifelong friends. Whether she's making introductions on social media or gathering people in a room, Keisha has this incredible gift for seeing exactly how people can lift each other up—and she absolutely loves making it happen."

— **Zee Slingsby,** Strategist Coach

"Keisha is a powerhouse! She has an incredible ability to lead her people and help them capture a message that really attracts the right type of audience. If you're reading this book and thinking about becoming a part of her tribe, 100% do it. She rocks."

— **Colin Boyd,** International Speaker,
Author and Sell From Stage Coach

"A powerful wake-up call for high-performing women who feel unfulfilled despite their success, Inevitable *reveals the hidden truth: the identity that got you here won't take you where you're meant to go next. With raw honesty and clarity, Keisha Leilani shows how shifting who you are, not just what you do, is the key to deeper fulfillment, influence, and lasting authority."*

— **Cris Cawley, CEO,** Game Changer Publishing

READ THIS FIRST

I appreciate your purchase. It doesn't go unnoticed.
Thank you for your support and for reading my book.
Let's connect!

Scan the QR Code Here:

FOREWORD

Watching Keisha build her career and life has been incredible. She is the kind of woman who sees opportunity where others see obstacles and then has the courage, discipline, and heart to go after it. She doesn't just dream big ideas; she brings them to life and turns them into real growth and sales. What makes Keisha truly special goes far beyond numbers or titles. She leads with intuition, confidence, and an unmatched work ethic, while still lifting everyone around her higher. She is the friend who believes in you before you believe in yourself, the boss who sets the standard, and the visionary who leads with fearless ambition.

This book is Keisha in written form.

It's honest, strategic, and motivating. It's for anyone who wants to build something meaningful, step into their power, and learn from someone who has done the work, taken the risks, and created success on her own terms. I couldn't be prouder to call her my friend, and I couldn't be more excited for you to learn from her through these pages.

— Kailynn Bowling, CEO

TABLE OF CONTENTS

INTRODUCTION

THE ILLUSION OF MOMENTUM

I'm not just a coach; I'm a mirror.

I'm a woman who has built power offline and is now called to help other powerful women express theirs online. I don't just build brands; I reintroduce brilliance.

So, how did I arrive at this point in my life?

What I didn't realize at the time was that my journey wasn't just about ambition or resilience; it was spiritual. Long before I had the language for alignment, I had faith. A quiet, steady knowing that there was a deeper truth guiding me, even when my life didn't reflect it yet. My faith became the compass I returned to again and again, especially in moments when success looked right on the outside but felt wrong in my spirit.

My journey began with my biological mother telling me I wouldn't amount to anything without the military. Deep down, I knew that wasn't true. Instead, I embraced entrepreneurship, helping women turn their tribulations into triumphs and their pain into power.

I built businesses, acquired skills, and did all the right things. It worked until it didn't. I reached a point where performance was profitable but not peaceful. I remember sitting at my laptop, staring at the revenue numbers on the screen, but feeling completely empty. My body and chest felt heavy and exhausted. I said to myself, *Why do I feel nothing?*

I didn't need a new plan at that moment. I needed permission to stop running from the truth.

On paper, I had built success, but inside, I felt empty, disconnected, like the life I was building didn't actually belong to me. It was in that silence, staring at my achievements, that the truth hit me: Profit without peace is just another form of prison. That's when I learned that alignment isn't optional; it's essential.

For me, alignment meant listening to God more closely than the noise of expectations, metrics, or applause.

A network marketing company I previously worked with was not fully authentic. Their demands, the tasks assigned to me, and the expectations placed on me consistently challenged my morals and values. My role lacked alignment. By compromising who I was and what I believed in, I compromised myself. It was by exiting this company that I was able to realign my personal values with my work.

That decision wasn't strategic. It was spiritual.

I kept meeting women who were once celebrated but now felt invisible. They weren't stuck in their businesses; they were stuck in a version of themselves that their brands no longer reflected.

Because when a woman finally tells herself the truth, everything she builds after that changes.

This isn't a book of strategies; it's a mirror, a model for your next level. I saw it in my clients: Brianna, Jessica, Maggie, and Emily. Though successful on paper, they suffocated in silence. They didn't need another marketing funnel; they needed a reintroduction to themselves.

This is for the woman who is the go-to expert in rooms filled with people she has outgrown. She has built a brand that whispers when it was meant to roar and has success that looks good on paper but doesn't feel fulfilling in her soul. She isn't confused; she's constrained. She doesn't need another funnel; she needs her message to finally land.

I have lived this evolution. I have coached women through it and witnessed the transformation that occurs when a woman reclaims her clarity, her voice, and her presence. I'm not offering theory; I'm offering transformation.

You will gain a new internal blueprint for scaling in alignment, tools to rebuild your brand based on presence, not pressure, permission to stop performing and start embodying your truth, messaging that matches your magnitude, a roadmap for showing up powerfully online, a recalibrated inner compass to evolve without starting over, and a playbook for becoming unforgettable, not just viral.

My hope is that you stop shrinking to fit outdated strategies, see your brilliance clearly, stop whispering, and start leading.

This book is the beginning of your becoming.

I know you're tired, not from doing too much but from engaging in what no longer fits. You're not lazy; you're not lost. You are exhausted from pretending to be aligned, from overperforming a version of yourself that is no longer true. This isn't burnout from output; it's burnout from the mask. And that's where our journey begins.

Let's talk about it.

CHAPTER 1

THE DISGUISED BURNOUT: EXPOSING THE ILLUSION

The disguised burnout is someone who is still posting online, still attending meetings, and even participating in Zoom calls. However, behind the scenes, she's feeling numb, not necessarily depressed, but disconnected. She tries tweaking her offers, changing the font, and writing new captions, yet nothing feels authentic to her anymore.

That little spark she once had is now flickering. She's beginning to resent the very thing she used to love, not because the work changed, but because she changed. The brand she built no longer recognizes who she is.

She appears successful but is silently drained.

I was exhausted from my work in the network marketing business. I was checking all the boxes and completing everything I needed to, but I didn't feel authentic when it came to what I truly wanted in my soul. I needed to find my voice and the ability to lead in a way that aligned with my mission and passion.

I remember being invited to my first women's mastermind with two of my best friends. I'll never forget sitting in a circle with a bunch of other entrepreneurial women and the host asking everyone why they were there. When it was my turn,

I felt the tickle in my throat of a cry about to start. My hands clenched in my lap, and my heart pounded so hard I could hear it in my ears.

The host of the event said, "Why don't you come up here?" She then prayed over me and told me God was using me and my story in a way I couldn't see yet. And then she asked, "What's the story only you can tell?"

I opened my mouth, but nothing came out. My throat tightened, and before I could stop myself, tears spilled over. It wasn't that I didn't have my own story; it was that I had lost it. I had been buried so deeply inside my ex's identity, his success, and his vision that my own felt overshadowed, so much so that I couldn't find it.

For years, I had been buried inside my ex's identity, his success, and his vision. I remember standing in the back of conference rooms while people lined up to shake his hand, take pics with him, ask him questions, and thank him for his leadership. I was right there, but it was like I was invisible. Smiles passed me by. Conversations skipped over me. Without even realizing it, I had shrunk into the shadows of someone else's spotlight.

That's why nothing came out when I tried to speak. My silence wasn't weakness; it was a sign of how much I'd been holding back. But something shifted that day, and the women who were there made me feel heard, seen, and understood. For the first time, I felt that what I had lived through mattered, not because it looked like anyone else's journey, but because it was mine.

During a season where I was hitting every external marker of success, helping clients achieve results, and gaining visibility, I would log off coaching calls feeling completely drained. It wasn't that I didn't care; it was that I was coaching from strategy rather than from a place of alignment with my true calling and purpose. I kept telling myself I was just tired, but what I was really feeling was misalignment. My content lacked energy, and it felt flat and unoriginal. My previous mission had become burdensome.

I recognized that I had built a business around a version of myself that no longer existed, and that was for the sake of others, instead of nurturing true alignment. The turning point came when I realized I didn't want to simplify the process; I wanted to reclaim my voice. I aspired to step into my authentic self, which would help me attract the clients I wanted to work with.

That was the day I stopped tweaking my approach and began to listen more to myself. I stopped comparing myself to others in the industry and started leading with my authentic calling.

I believe that burnout manifests differently for different women, especially for those who are already successful. For some, burnout is internal. They carry a quiet resentment of their schedules and the grind they've created.

This can look like high-functioning burnout, where a woman cancels meetings and dreads deadlines but simultaneously resents the pace she has set. Instead of falling apart, her breakdown may appear as hyperperformance. She may over-deliver, over-edit, and over-compensate for a brand that no longer aligns with her true self.

When a woman's success is built around achievement, exhaustion can occur, though it's often misinterpreted as reaching the next level. What she truly needs isn't more structure; it's a safe space to land within her messaging, voice, and authentic self, which fosters genuine alignment.

It's crucial to understand the difference between internal alignment and external achievement and momentum. Alignment means connecting with the deep-rooted soul mission that you intuitively know will guide you to your goals.

In my experience, busy women can often feel off track. If you ask them what they are building, they may struggle to tell you. Momentum is easy to manufacture, but alignment is not. They might be focused on content calendars rather than the true clarity that comes from being on track with their soul's purpose and aligning with what they are divinely called to create and accomplish.

When a woman's brand is built solely on her skills rather than her true identity, she becomes more of a technician than a genuine thought leader in her field. She achieves results that lead to increased visibility, but without the vitality that comes from true alignment. She may appear to be doing well, but internally, she is grappling with who she is becoming. While she needs both elements, she currently possesses only one.

The old version of her continues to run the business. Often, she outgrows her offers, voice, and identity after achieving financial success. Her sales funnel may still operate effectively, but she dislikes discussing the offer. Why? Because that offer, voice, and positioning were created by a past version of herself who no longer fits the current landscape. While she attempts to scale through strategy, she finds that strategy alone, without her authentic voice, leads to suffocation. She has evolved, but her business hasn't kept pace.

Every time she tries to optimize, she is really just avoiding the need for reintroduction. What she truly needs is not a new offer; she needs to embrace the woman who now sells that offer. The danger lies not in the risk of losing relevance but in remaining loyal to a version of herself that she has outgrown.

Alignment feels different from misalignment. It can change how she shows up, not just what she does. Being aligned doesn't mean that everything is easy; rather, it energizes her even during tough times. In alignment, content flows naturally and effortlessly. She genuinely wants to engage with her work because it resonates with her. After sales calls, she feels invigorated rather than depleted, and she eagerly looks forward to the next call because it aligns with who she is.

Misalignment, on the other hand, can be subtle. It manifests as avoidance of visibility, a need for excessive tweaking of things that used to come easily, and a feeling of performing a message rather than living it. Alignment doesn't shout; it whispers.

But once she hears that whisper, she can no longer ignore it.

Her 2.0 is calling. I remember what it felt like to evolve into my 2.0 identity. I had to let go of a lot, even when it seemed to be working. I had to change parts of my voice, brand, and offers before new success could arrive. Part of that process involved embracing the idea that my mess could become my message.

When I stepped into my 2.0, it wasn't glamorous, let me tell you. It meant saying no to many things that still paid well but completely drained my soul and spirit. I even deleted a six-figure program I had already built, not because it wasn't functioning, but because it no longer resonated with who I was becoming.

When this transition occurs, and you truly step into alignment with the identity of your evolving self, you begin to examine other aspects of your business or life that no longer serve your deeper essence. I had to let go of a version of myself that needed to prove I could do it all, which was challenging. I had to stop chasing validation and start pursuing my voice and intuition, the kind that didn't whisper strategies but roared in any room I entered.

The moment I embraced this shift, I felt a transformation. I entered an energetic space that aligned with my voice and intuition. When I walked into a room, people could feel that magnetic energy. My evolution wasn't about building more; it was about becoming more of myself and being a brand and voice through which others could see themselves and realize they could also embark on this journey.

Unfortunately, before this realization, burnout led me to quit multiple times. I've been an entrepreneur since I was sixteen and experienced burnout repeatedly, which left me feeling muted. Clarity, when it finally arrived, was the catalyst that helped me regain my boldness and sense of self. I realized that I was never tired from work itself; I was tired from laboring around my true self and the person I wanted to become.

That shift didn't begin with just implementing a funnel; it started with a decision to stop marketing in ways that felt misaligned or as if I were trying to fit in with others.

Mindset traps often kept me feeling small. Thoughts like, *Don't mess with what's working,* and *What if they don't follow the new version of me?* plagued my mind. The truth, however, is that my message required me to expand, not shrink. If my message demands that I shrink, I don't want that sale.

I strive to lean into this realization as often as I can. Clarity returned the moment I stopped performing and began embodying my true self.

I like to conduct a weekly internal audit, taking time to ask myself deep questions that serve as a mirror for introspection. These questions include:

- What am I tired of that I haven't spoken aloud?
- Where am I still trying to prove something I've already earned?
- Which offers, platforms, or strategies no longer feel authentic to me?
- When did I stop trusting myself to know what's next?

These are not surface-level prompts; they are pivotal questions that lead to insights I already know the answers to.

To become the next version of yourself, you need to feel safe enough to express your true feelings. Many women attempt to solve burnout simply by resting, but you can't rest your way out of misalignment. When misalignment isn't a pacing issue, it's a problem of presence. You might feel exhausted, not because you're doing too much, but because you're engaging in the wrong activities as an outdated version of yourself.

This is why clarity is essential before making changes to funnels, launches, or new offers, or before reworking your strategy. If your path is still unclear, no marketing plan will effectively convert because your energy reflects your state of mind, and confusion will always seep into your brand.

Having clarity and a solid foundation is critical, as it guides you toward leading with truth and alignment. I once worked with a seven-figure entrepreneur, Brianna, who appeared successful on the outside but felt exhausted, indecisive, and stuck internally. She didn't require a complete overhaul of her business; she needed clarity.

Once her brand and business realigned with her evolving self, everything changed. Her energy improved, her team became more cohesive, her clients responded positively, and her revenue increased. Despite her impressive track record, she felt disconnected and that her content was forced. She was like a hamster on a wheel, struggling to keep up with external expectations.

When we started collaborating, Brianna needed assistance in rebuilding her business in a way that resonated with her true self. I helped her reconnect with who she genuinely was and strip away the outdated persona she had outgrown, and we recalibrated her messaging to reflect her authentic self.

The outcome? While her offers remained the same, her energy transformed. Her direct messages were revitalized without any promotional effort, and her clients remarked that they finally sounded like her. Her team no longer waited for direction; her clarity restored their vision. She began attracting the type of clients she desired, and it felt fulfilling to her soul.

What she truly needed was permission to evolve into her divine mission and purpose. This is where the real reset begins. I use a four-step recalibration framework to help those who feel drained without understanding why.

It's called **REAL**:

1. **R**ecognize the Misalignment: Identify where you might be succeeding but secretly feel diminished. What no longer resonates with you, even if it is still effective?
2. **E**xtract the Truth: What truths have you been avoiding to maintain peace with your clients, audience, or even your former self? Where are you pretending everything is fine when you're actually finished?
3. **A**lign with Who You Are Now: If you allowed yourself to evolve, what would change? Your messaging, your presence, your pricing? What version of yourself would stop managing and start embodying?
4. **L**ead from Your New Frequency: Stop waiting for validation. Start expressing yourself as the future version of you that your next level depends on. Leadership is no longer about doing more but about being more: more honest, more present, and more powerful.

What I appreciate about this framework is its energetic nature; it focuses on internal shifts before any external strategy changes. Without this reset, you run the risk of repeating the same cycle of misalignment, just packaged differently.

This isn't just about burnout. It's your brilliance asking for better alignment. You're not tired because you can't keep up;

you're tired because you're still pretending to be a version of yourself that you've already outgrown.

So, here's a challenge for you: take out a journal and complete this writing prompt, no filters, no fluff.

Fill in the blank:
The part of me I've been protecting to be successful is ______.

Now fill in the blank again:
But the version of me who's ready to lead now is __________.

The moment you write that down is the moment you start to return to your true self.

Chapter Summary: Key Takeaways

- Burnout doesn't always look like collapse. Many women experience **high-functioning or disguised burnout**, where they remain productive and visible while feeling numb, disconnected, and misaligned internally.
- Exhaustion often stems not from doing too much but from **operating as a version of yourself you've already outgrown**, especially when success is built on external achievement rather than internal alignment.
- When a brand or business no longer reflects who you are becoming, **tweaking strategy, content, or offers won't fix the problem; reconnection** with your voice will.
- True alignment is rooted in **identity and purpose**, not momentum; momentum can be manufactured, but alignment must be embodied.
- Misalignment shows up subtly through resentment, avoidance, over-editing, loss of creative energy, and performing a message rather than living it.

- Evolution requires courage; letting go of offers, strategies, or identities that still "work" but no longer resonate is often necessary to step into your next level.
- You cannot rest your way out of misalignment; **clarity and presence**, not more structure or hustle, are what restore energy and vitality.
- Leadership shifts when you stop seeking validation and start **embodying the version of yourself your future requires.** Your energy, not your effort, becomes the signal.
- Sustainable success begins with internal recalibration: recognizing misalignment, extracting truth, aligning with who you are now, and leading from that new frequency.

CHAPTER 2

ALIGNING WITH YOUR 2.0

Many successful women are often celebrated for roles, achievements, and behaviors that no longer serve them. They are the ones who always show up, make it look easy, carry the team, and deliver results. But how are they rewarded for remaining versions of themselves that they have outgrown? The weight that comes with their success often goes unseen.

Their consistency becomes a cage, their excellence turns into expectation, and their leadership feels like an obligation. They receive praise for being versions of themselves that they secretly cannot stand anymore.

The cost of remaining loyal to a former identity is steep, as it drains them of clarity, creativity, health, and peace. Every time they choose to be who they used to be instead of who they feel called to become, they lose that clarity, creativity, and the magic that once made them so magnetic.

The cost isn't just emotional; it's also energetic and financial. If a successful woman is creating offers, she's likely building ones she doesn't want to deliver. She may be shrinking her brand to keep existing clients comfortable and leading a business that no longer excites her. The real fear many of these women face is *What if I lose the audience I've built? What if they don't understand the new me? What if I evolve and it doesn't work?*

Have you ever experienced this fear, felt unable to evolve, lacked clarity and creativity, struggled with your health, and perhaps even lost your peace? There comes a point when success no longer feels sacred. I remember a time when I was growing my brand and myself, but my brand didn't reflect that growth. I would walk into rooms, and people would only recognize the woman I used to be, not the woman I had become.

Then I saw a post about myself that caused me to recognize how out of touch I had become, not because it was unflattering, but because it was no longer true. That moment made it clear that I had to risk being misunderstood in order to be seen for who I truly am. Once I let go of the applause that kept me confined, everything began to expand: my voice, my offers, my vision, all of it. I started to feel like myself again.

In my early days in network marketing, although I experienced success, I felt a significant disconnect. There were times when I was performing to please others, dictated by the movements and expectations established by higher-tier teammates that didn't truly align with who I was. There were behind-the-scenes realities that were also misaligned with my authenticity, my heart, and what I stand for in this world.

I found it challenging to step into those rooms and engage with those women, knowing that there were unspoken issues that truly affected my soul, alignment, mission, and vision for success in life. I strive to become a prominent presence in any room I enter. Many people compete to lead, but I prefer to coach others to stop competing and start leading.

Competing through comparison, people-pleasing, or chasing trends traps you in a mindset of misery. I always say, "Comparison is misery." When you compare yourself to others, you limit your potential and hinder your ability to thrive and reach the next level of success, whatever that looks like for you. To embody your authority and leadership, you must stay in your lane and focus on your path. This approach to competition is different from what others may do.

It's no longer about copying someone else; it's about contouring. What I mean by this is that when someone lowers her prices to compete or overeducates herself out of fear that her elegance will be seen as emptiness, she is no longer being true to herself. Making tweaks to one's offers to seem more relatable only detracts from authenticity.

True leadership is about ceasing to manage how others perceive you and starting to own your presence. Instead of asking, *Will they like this?* you should be asking, *Is this aligned with who I have become?* This question will attract the ideal clients and customers who resonate with your true essence.

Leadership is trusting that your full presence acts as both a magnet and your marketing. That realization is powerful. For me, becoming "the name in the room" means embodying who I truly am, exhibiting my presence, and aligning my actions with my words in a genuine way. Being recognized as "the name" doesn't necessarily mean being loud, but being clear and authentic.

When you are "the name in the room," your name is whispered in conversations you haven't even initiated. Your content exudes authority before you even speak, and people feel your brand's energy before engaging with you. You don't need more exposure; you need to stand firm in your evolution.

I remember a time when I spoke about social media in a large setting. I was able to stand out because I embodied that presence and energy we discussed earlier. People felt that energy, and it inspired them to take action in their businesses or personal lives. I became "the name in the room" because of the energy I created in that moment.

So, the real question isn't *how do I get seen*? But rather, *am I showing up as the version of myself that the room is already seeking?*

Authenticity, relatability, and helping others see themselves in your journey are crucial. When they think, *If she can do it, so can I,* they begin to recognize you as "the name in the room."

Have you ever felt like you were the name in the room?

Next, I want to discuss how my focus shifted from merely building a business to creating a true legacy. This required deep reflection on my legacy and values: what they were, how they changed, and how they needed to change. I also had to consider whether my brand and messaging needed an overhaul to genuinely build that legacy.

For me, the business question is, *"How do I make this work?* But the legacy question is, *What was I born to build?* These are two completely different inquiries. When you shift your focus to legacy building, your values become louder than your visibility.

You begin to say "no" more often without feeling guilty. You stop following trends and start determining what is genuinely true. This is the moment when your strategy evolves into something more profound: embodiment.

When you realize that templates won't create what you were uniquely meant to bring into the world, you understand that legacy isn't about being loud; it's about lasting impact. A true legacy outlasts current trends, transcends algorithms, and operates in full energetic alignment.

When you lead with the intention of building a legacy, whether for your family, business, or life in general, the energy shifts. This energy translates both online and offline, which is where your messaging begins to align more closely with your brand, values, and mission. You shift from simply building a business to creating a meaningful legacy, leading from identity rather than strategy.

In this space, strategy is often overemphasized. The message is usually "You have to do it this way or that way." While strategy does play a role, I believe it's only a small part of what can propel you to the next level of success.

If you focus on your identity, as we discussed in earlier chapters, you can tap into that internal drive or soul craving, a God-given gift or talent you're meant to share. When you live out your God-given purpose, your identity naturally informs your strategy.

I remember a time in my life when I led strictly with strategy rather than my identity. I achieved some level of success, but it came at a cost. I found myself questioning whether I was doing things the right way.

At one point, I became obsessed with doing everything correctly. I chased every hack, followed every trend, and posted at the "perfect" time. I got so caught up in strategy that I lost sight of my identity and the reasons behind my actions.

When I first started coaching, I tried to replicate what others were doing on social media. Digital marketing was booming, and I felt pressured to learn all the strategies and trends. I created content for superficial reasons, seeking likes instead of focusing on my true legacy.

Initially, this approach worked. My follower count soared from zero to 56,000 in just three months. Engagement levels skyrocketed, with people signing up for my digital products and my reels garnering millions of views. But soon, everything plateaued. This was a shock to me, as I had become addicted to rapid engagement and growth.

The issue wasn't the strategy; it was that I was building on a shaky sense of self. I was visible but not genuinely seen. I was selling, but not from the depths of my soul. I was trying to optimize a voice I hadn't yet fully claimed. Instead of embracing my God-given potential and purpose, I was conforming to what others were doing, trying to fit their mold of success.

The real shift happened not when I got smarter but when I became braver. I started putting myself out there, living in alignment with my true self. When I stopped trying to follow formulas and began expressing what only I could say, I became undeniable. This journey of recognizing the significance of my messaging and the legacy I wanted to leave was vital in my evolution towards the next version of myself.

I began attracting more of my ideal dream clients, customers, and audience, not just seeking likes, engagement, or followers. This shift occurred when I started leading from my identity rather than from strategy. Have you ever had a moment in your life when you were leading with strategy instead of your true identity? If so, when was that?

An internal conflict can arise between who you used to be and who you are becoming. These voices or pressures of expectation can sometimes hold you back. There has always been a tension between the known identity, the one that helped you achieve success, and the emerging identity that requires risk and the possibility of being misunderstood.

The old version of you might say, *Don't rock the boat. Stay where it's safe. This is working*. In contrast, the woman you are becoming is ready to stop dimming her light, stop filtering herself, and build her business and voice based on her vision, not someone else's strategy.

The truth is, staying loyal to an outdated version of yourself may preserve your audience, but it will cost you your power. This is crucial because many voices, pressures, and expectations can pull you backward. You cannot reach the next phase of becoming your best self, your highest self, and fulfilling your purpose if you remain attached to a past version of yourself.

While that version may feel safe and comfortable, I strive to help my clients become uncomfortable, as that's where true growth occurs. It's an opportunity for learning and development.

Now, I'd like to encourage you to conduct an identity audit. Reflect deeply using the following prompts to uncover your truth:

1. What version of me am I currently known for, and does she still feel authentic?
2. What does the next version of me believe, say, charge towards, and walk into?
3. Which conversations or offers no longer excite me?
4. Where am I shrinking to stay safe, even when I'm ready to be seen?

Take some time to sit with these questions.

These are more than just reflections; they are reintroductions. This is an important concept.

Reintroduction involves high-level women who already have a successful brand or offering but feel misaligned, muted, or bored behind the scenes. They fear that letting go of their existing brand might cost them credibility, but when they choose to reintroduce themselves, everything shifts.

In the first chapter, I mentioned Brianna, who had built a successful brand and business but no longer felt like it aligned with her true self. When she came to me, she had already achieved what most people dream of: a seven-figure business offline. She was well-respected in her town, very successful, and in high demand. However, online, she felt like a stranger in a space that didn't see her. Although she wasn't starting from scratch, that's how the online world made her feel.

Every strategy she tried was aimed at beginners. The advice she received felt diluted, and the messaging didn't reflect her depth.

She didn't need more noise; she needed a mirror. Together, we stripped away the strategies that caused her to shrink. We helped her reconnect with the woman behind the business, clarified her essence, and reclaimed her new identity. She began communicating from her soul rather than scripting from fear.

What happened next was remarkable: her energy shifted. She became confident in what she had to offer again. Her brand spoke even louder without needing to shout. She began attracting dream clients, women who were ready to be led by someone who didn't just have success but embodied it.

Brianna didn't need a funnel; she needed a frequency. Once she tapped into that, the right clients found her without the chase.

Let's talk about a framework moment: the identity shift. Many women try to scale their strategies, but what truly fuels next-level success is an identity shift.

Here's how the identity shift loop works:

1. Old Identity: This is the person you've known, perhaps a done-for-you expert, coach, or behind-the-scenes fixer.
2. Trigger Moment: This often feels like burnout, boredom, or frustration with content or clients. You realize *I've outgrown this role, but I'm still being seen through it.*
3. Friction Phase: You might think, *The brand works, but I don't feel like me anymore.* Your strategy feels off, and sales are down. You start questioning everything.
4. Reclamation Shift: You begin to ask yourself, *What would change if I stopped performing and started embodying?* This could involve reclaiming your power, voice, and presence.
5. Reintroduction: You now confidently express, *This is who I am now,* and you're unafraid to be seen as this new version of yourself. You speak, sell, and lead differently in the market.

I want you to consider this: you don't need to throw everything away. You just need to stop building around the woman you once were and start scaling from who you truly are now.

The identity shift isn't a rebrand; it's a return, a reintroduction, a rooted decision to scale from your soul rather than simply from strategy.

When you step into who you are and who you are becoming, your message becomes more magnetic. More people are drawn to what you have to say because they see themselves reflected in your messaging. This connection helps build trust, making them more inclined to invest in your products and programs. They want to be part of your social media presence and your world because your messaging magnetizes them.

Once you own your voice, your audience listens in a different way. An energetic shift occurs when people feel this new energy and frequency of who you are and what you can contribute to the world. They are attracted to listen to and engage with you, and they respond differently.

This shift helps you redefine your programs, offers, identity, and rebranding. It's crucial to step into this space, where using your voice and branding creates an identity that attracts the right people, those you want to work with and who want to work with you.

Behind the scenes of my transformation, there was a quiet but defining moment when I realized I could no longer lead from the version of myself that the market was accustomed to or from the brand I had built in the industry.

The evidence was there: my income was solid, and my online presence was curated and edited. I was creating content based on strategy when I was called to embody true leadership. I was giving information when I needed to provide clarity, and the more I adhered to the formula, the more disconnected I felt from the women I was supposed to lead.

So, I paused and asked myself a different question: *What version of me would I hire at the highest level right now?* The answer didn't stem from more training or tactics; it came from a deeper truth.

I reintroduced myself publicly, not with a flashy announcement but through a subtle shift. My words became bolder, my content cleaner, and my offers aligned with my wisdom. That single energetic shift completely changed how others perceived me. Clients began reaching out through my DMs, not because I was selling more, but because I was embodying more.

What changed were my boundaries, brand voice, and confidence to engage in higher-caliber conversations without over-explaining. The lesson here is that reintroduction is the new reinvention, and it begins the moment you stop waiting for permission to be powerful.

Many people miss this opportunity because they get caught up in what everyone else is doing, following trends and formulas created by others. Instead, it's vital to give yourself permission to own your truth, your voice, and your brand and to acknowledge the messy and difficult aspects of your journey in a way that draws people in. They will feel a sense of trust and connection, wanting to be part of your world.

You've already evolved; now it's time to announce it. You don't need to prove your worth; you need to own your presence. Your next level isn't waiting for permission; it's waiting for you to embody it.

Stop curating content for a version of your brand you've outgrown. Stop letting strategy overshadow your spirit. Respect the version of you that built it, but command the room with the version of you that is leading it now. You are no longer just playing the game; you are the name.

Here's a journal prompt I'd like you to consider: What version of yourself are you still performing out of fear, comfort, or loyalty? The version of yourself that you are becoming embraces certain opportunities and rejects others. If you were to embody that version today, what would you express, promote, or choose to stop justifying? It's time to draw the line, step into that identity, and allow the world to adapt accordingly.

Declare it in your own words:

"The version of me I've outgrown is ______________________ (the one who second-guessed her power and waited for permission). I'm no longer shrinking to be seen. I'm ________________ (rooted, radiant, and ready for everything aligned with my next level). If I were to publicly reintroduce myself today, I would say __________________________. Let this be the day my presence gets louder than my strategy."

The version of me I've outgrown is **the woman who kept proving her worth instead of fully owning her authority** (the one who second-guessed her power and waited for permission).

I'm no longer shrinking to be seen. I'm **anchored in faith, grounded in leadership, and fully available for the level of impact I know I'm here to create**.

If I were to publicly reintroduce myself today, I would say **I guide high-level women entrepreneurs into the identity and leadership required to hold their next level of visibility, influence, and income.**

Let this be the day my presence gets louder than my strategy.

I believe that when we seek external validation, we can find ourselves in a challenging position. I remember a time in network marketing when I was chasing rewards, money, and other external factors. The problem with this approach is that it often leads to misalignment: the product may not be right, the team may not be a good fit, or the training may not be effective. This can create significant internal conflict.

Intuitively, we recognize this disconnect. We might feel that what we are doing doesn't align with our true purpose or potential. Instead, it often feels like we're pursuing quick satisfaction based on external factors. We think back to experiences in our childhood where we didn't receive the validation we needed. As a result, we might chase these external achievements to prove our worth and feel significant.

However, staying aligned with who you truly are can be much more fulfilling. When you focus on both your internal values and external goals, something magical happens. You start to live in a way that resonates deeply with your true self, and others can sense that energy. This creates a magnetic quality that draws people to you.

When you start chasing the money, the fame, the rewards, and all that, you start to get further away from your God and the truth. I see female entrepreneurs who hustle from a place of pressure, not purpose, chasing validation, overdelivering, and pretending everything's fine just to maintain an image.

Honestly, I stopped following others' products, programs, and social media reels. Being highly competitive is a struggle for me, and I realized I was doing it constantly by comparing myself to others.

My entire life has been shaped by this competitiveness, but everything changed when I started leading with truth, authenticity, and energy. I began attracting people who shared my alignment, goals, vision, and mission. When I was caught up in competition, I was much harder on myself and often doubted my abilities.

The turning point for me was when I decided to stop watching other people's content. I work in digital marketing and social media, so it's easy to get caught up in what others are doing. This can lead to feelings similar to those I had when dealing with my ex, thinking my story should mirror someone else's. That left me feeling small instead of empowered, powerless instead of thriving.

When I watch reels or read emails from people who inspire me, I approach them with a different mindset. I think *I can learn something from them,* rather than viewing it as a competition. I recognize that I can approach things in a way that's aligned with my voice and brand. Their success is different from mine, and that's perfectly okay.

I believe that competition can be damaging not only to yourself but also to the overall energy in the world. It often leads to feelings of inadequacy. Instead of competing, I encourage you to connect with entrepreneurs who inspire you.

Focus on collaboration rather than competition. It may feel uncomfortable, especially if you're comparing yourself to someone else or trying to emulate them. But why not take the brave step of contacting that person and proposing a collaborative project? What's the worst that could happen? This approach allows you to move away from competition and toward collaboration, potentially creating a mutually beneficial partnership.

Chapter Summary: Key Takeaways

- Many successful women are praised for **versions of themselves they have already outgrown**, and over time, that praise can become a **cage** that drains their **clarity, creativity, health, and peace**.

- Remaining loyal to an **outdated identity** carries real **emotional, energetic, and financial costs**, often leading to **offers, messaging, and leadership roles** that no longer feel aligned or fulfilling.
- The **fear of evolving**, losing an audience, being misunderstood, or disrupting what "works" causes many women to perform instead of being fully **seen**.
- True leadership is not about **managing perception**, **copying others**, or **chasing trends**. It is about **owning your presence** and asking whether your actions align with **who you have become**.
- Being **"the name in the room"** is less about visibility and more about **embodiment**. Your **energy, clarity, and authenticity** become your most powerful marketing tools.
- **Strategy alone** cannot sustain long-term success. When **identity leads and strategy follows**, momentum becomes **magnetic rather than forced**.
- Growth often requires an **identity shift**, not a rebrand or reinvention, but a **reintroduction** that honors who you are now rather than who the market expects you to be.
- Staying attached to a **past version of yourself** may feel safe, but it will **cost you your power**. Evolution demands **discomfort, courage, and a willingness to lead without permission**.
- The next level of success comes when you **stop competing**, **stop shrinking**, and **stop performing**, and instead **scale your business, voice, and legacy** from **alignment, truth, and embodied authority**.

CHAPTER 3

MINDSET RECALIBRATION: THE MYTH OF THE MINDSET-PROOF WOMAN

Money can change people. Are entitlement and power filling you up or eating you alive?

You need clarity about who you are meant to be and your God-given purpose. I've watched people become distracted by shiny objects, only to lose everything in a short period of time. That experience can leave lasting scars and an inability to be successful again. I want to emphasize that mindset challenges don't simply disappear with money.

Let's be honest: the higher you rise, the better the mask you wear. You may have accolades, income, and a supportive team, but you might feel you lack the permission to admit, "I'm stuck, and I'm tired. I've outgrown this version of myself, but I'm scared to say it out loud." High-achieving women don't avoid mindset work because they are too evolved; they avoid it because they fear what the truth may cost them.

In elite circles, there's a dangerous myth: "I shouldn't be dealing with this anymore." The reality is that mindset work isn't about beginning; it's about becoming. I believe that mindset myths predominantly exist in elite environments.

Internal misalignment can manifest in various ways, even at the top. Sometimes, it manifests as overthinking despite expertise, playing smaller than your platform allows, or self-editing in the presence of other high achievers. You might find yourself downplaying your brilliance to fit in with rooms you've already outgrown.

In this situation, you might be questioning your authority, even when your track record screams credibility. You may be crafting content for the algorithm instead of engaging in genuine conversations with the women who are eager for your leadership. You appear successful, but it feels like you're merely going through the motions. You've built your dream, yet it no longer feels like yours.

I remember a time when I was riding the public wave of success while privately battling self-doubt. I achieved milestones and received rewards and opportunities that others were still journaling about. Yet, I kept asking myself, *Am I allowed to be this clear? Will they still follow me if I don't soften my edge?*

What I discovered is that I wasn't stuck in strategy. I was trapped in an identity I had already outgrown. This epiphany didn't come from another mentor; it came from being radically honest with myself. I didn't need more tactics or strategy; I needed a new truth to stand on. I had outgrown my default settings.

A successful woman might be running a six- or seven-figure business, yet her mindset reflects only a six-figure belief. It doesn't quite add up, trying to maintain a seven-figure brand on a six-figure mindset. Such outdated beliefs can be burdensome, telling her to be grateful for what's working, to stay consistent even when it's draining, or to avoid rocking the boat. But here's the hard truth: what helped her reach this point will lead to burnout if she doesn't upgrade her internal settings.

Sometimes, an outdated mindset can manifest in women like her. This may include seeking permission before making bold moves, over-delivering to justify her prices, struggling to ask for support or rest, and shrinking in rooms where she should be taking the lead. She might find herself asking for advice when she already knows the answer. Additionally, she might tend to over-coach and over-explain in an effort to validate her pricing.

She avoids rest because she feels she hasn't earned it and lowers her voice in situations where she should be the keynote speaker. This behavior isn't rooted in humility; rather, it stems from an identity that no longer serves her.

There was a time in my life when I ran a successful network marketing business with a team that relied on me all the time. I was chasing success to demonstrate what it could look like for them and their families.

This pursuit turned into a trap for me, as my mindset didn't keep pace with my growth. Even though I was experiencing success, I held on to limiting beliefs, suggesting that my team couldn't achieve the same level of success due to their own limiting beliefs and challenges.

But the truth? I was terrified of slowing down. I worried that if I did, the whole thing would fall apart. My momentum grew so fast that my mindset couldn't keep up. Even as I hit new ranks and income goals, I started to believe a lie, that maybe my team couldn't duplicate what I did, that they were either intimidated by my success or they already doubted that they could have what I had created.

Looking back, I realize it wasn't about them. It was about me trying to prove my worth through their results. Network marketing taught me a lot about leadership but even more about alignment. Now I don't chase success to be an example. I build from a place of peace, alignment, and overflow because that's what I want the women I lead to experience, too.

Motivation once fueled me, but it could never sustain me. What truly changed everything was evolving my mindset because, let's be real, if you don't have real meaning behind it, you become burned out.

That's where the difference between motivation and recalibration comes in. Motivation urges you to push harder, while recalibration calls you to realign with your true self. One is about force; the other is about flow. The moment I stopped chasing momentum and started honoring alignment, everything in my life and business began to shift.

The successful woman doesn't need hype; she needs new default beliefs. At this level, she doesn't require another vision board.

What she needs is new programming. Recalibration means releasing the hustle, reclaiming her "why," and letting go of the rules she never fully agreed to. It's about refusing to prove herself anymore and choosing to own her identity.

Mindset recalibration at this level isn't about journaling affirmations or listening to a podcast while on the treadmill. It's about sitting down. It's about facing the version of yourself that got you to this point and having the courage to no longer let her lead. She served you well; she built the foundation, but she doesn't get to run the empire.

This is deep work, the kind that makes you question the blueprint upon which your success is built. That blueprint was designed for survival, approval, and acceptance from spaces that weren't meant for you.

Now it's time to rewrite your identity beliefs, those subconscious codes that say, *I need to work harder to earn more, Success means sacrifice,* or *If I rest, I lose momentum.*

You don't just challenge those beliefs; you replace them with truths that align with your upgraded identity. Ease is earned. Presence converts. You don't hustle; you lead.

Next, you recognize inherited narratives, not just from your upbringing but also the unspoken rules observed in your industry, from mentors, the community around you, and your culture.

These include ideas like "Stay humble," "Don't ruffle feathers," and "Be strategic, not emotional." You begin to realize that those rules were never yours, and they certainly don't define your legacy.

Ultimately, recalibration requires you to learn how to lead yourself through reinvention, not with more tasks to complete but with deeper self-trust. This means making bold moves before the plan is fully formed. It involves saying no to strategies that don't feel aligned, even if they're effective for others. It's about owning a voice that has evolved beyond what your current brand reflects.

This is the point where many women plateau, not due to a lack of strategy but because they haven't recalibrated their sense of identity. It's time for an internal audit.

Let's be honest: high-achieving women don't burn out because they're weak; they burn out because they're over-performing based on an outdated identity.

Here are some prompts for your next-level mindset questions. These aren't surface-level journal prompts; they are identity-level confrontations that elevate your highest self to the forefront.

- What do I believe I have to sacrifice to earn more? Perhaps it's time, peace, health, or relationships.
- Where am I still proving that I deserve to be here? Am I over-delivering to justify my pricing?
- What old story is playing on repeat, silently influencing my decisions? Who taught me that I can't have wealth and well-being?
- If I were leading from my highest self, what would I release immediately?
- Am I saying yes to work that no longer excites me just to appear useful?

Proving yourself is a prison. You don't need permission to lead. Your highest self isn't waiting for alignment; she embodies alignment.

Let me tell you about Jessica. On paper, she was an ideal client: highly regarded in her industry, known for her expertise, with impressive results, a strong reputation, and a wide reach.

But behind the scenes, she felt stuck. It wasn't because her offer was flawed or her audience had vanished; it was because her belief system hadn't evolved alongside her business. She kept tweaking her offers and funnel, revamping her branding, and testing new pricing. However, the real block was internal, not external.

Every time she attempted to step into her next level, she would shrink back. She feared being too much, sounding too certain, or charging too boldly. What she truly needed wasn't more strategy; she needed permission to lead like the woman she had already become.

So, we did the real work, the work that most high-achieving women tend to avoid. We recalibrated her core beliefs. We unpacked her need to prove herself, polish her image, and shrink back. We anchored her in her truth: she wasn't asking for a seat at the table; she was building her own.

The transformation was not gradual; it was immediate. Her voice became louder, not in volume but in conviction. Her content resonated differently, fueled by undeniable energy. While her offer remained the same, her presence shifted, becoming a magnet for her dream clients. Clients she once felt compelled to nurture into a sale began applying to work with her, paying in full and asking to be led.

Opportunities that had previously seemed out of reach started to present themselves without her having to chase them. Here's the surprising part: her launch revenue doubled without her adding more strategies. It wasn't about the copy; it was about the clarity.

Her frequency finally matched her authority, creating what I call the mindset recalibration loop. This isn't just fluff; it's frequency work. Mindset recalibration isn't about mantras but about interrupting the autopilot that runs your business behind the scenes.

I teach it like this: there's the trigger, the thought, and the truth. The trigger is a moment that pulls you out of your power. The thought is the unconscious belief it activates, and the truth is the recalibrated belief that anchors you back into leadership. You aren't just changing your mind; you're reprogramming your identity.

Has there been a moment in your life when you attempted to or successfully reprogrammed your identity? What did that look like?

Here are some ways you can use the mindset loop to address business-specific challenges:

One is the visibility block. The trigger could be seeing another woman thriving online, which might lead you to doubt your own voice. You might think, *Maybe I'm falling behind. Perhaps they're more legitimate than I am.* The truth, however, is that your power isn't about performance; it's about embodiment. You don't compete; you command. This illustrates how you can integrate the loop to shift your perspective on the visibility block.

Another example is the sales slump. In this case, the trigger might be launching a new product that doesn't sell out immediately. You might think, *Maybe I need to lower the price*, or *Perhaps no one wants this*. The reality is that your offer is intended for women who are ready to rise, and adopting a mindset of *I'm not here to beg; I'm here to build bold results* is key.

Your offer hasn't failed; rather, your belief has wavered, and your audience sensed that.

These two examples are effective for transforming your mindset and energy. When you change the way you show up, it influences how your audience engages with you, which attracts your ideal clients and creates a positive energy around your offers. The mindset loop moves from mere inspiration to a strategy of internal leadership. It's not just about being more positive; it's about cultivating powerful thinking.

Reclaiming thought leadership involves recalibrating your mindset, unlocking your potential, and turning inner work into external impact. When a woman recalibrates her mindset at this level, several things shift.

Her voice becomes sharper, shedding any fluff or fillers. She no longer says what is expected; she speaks her truth. Her content evolves from simple how-to guides to impactful messages of affirmation. She stops writing for likes and starts leading with a focus on legacy.

Her energy shifts from cautious to catalytic, capturing people's attention. They stop scrolling and start screenshotting, not because she's louder, but because she's clear. She's not just visible; she's undeniable. What sets her apart is that she's not quoting someone else's framework; she's embodying her own.

When you reclaim this type of leadership in your business and your offers, you become more aligned. Your voice becomes bolder, louder, and more authentic to who you are. Your beliefs shine through the content you create in your marketing, generating energy, movement, and momentum around you. This attracts the ideal clients you want to work with.

It's not about merely being visible; it's about being undeniable through your own voice and messaging that draws in your dream clients. Some mindset shifts have helped me become not just visible but undeniable, and I've seen these changes in my business.

When I stopped over-explaining, over-delivering, and over-performing to earn authority, I began to own my frequency, my unique frameworks, and my feminine power. That's when I noticed everything changed. Clients didn't just hire me; they felt more aligned with me.

I developed a coaching method called the Aligned Audience Method. I created this method because, early in my digital journey, I focused too much on creating content that mimicked what others were doing, which didn't align with me. It took me about three or four months to step into my voice and identity in this space because it can get overwhelming.

Everyone is trying to figure things out, and it can become cloudy. So, I shifted to doing things that felt more aligned with my true self. I started attracting my ideal, aligned clients, people like me who wanted to be part of my movement.

This shift wasn't about strategy; it was about sovereignty. That's when I stopped being just an option and became the only choice that made sense.

Closing Charge

To all the successful women out there, I just want to say, "Sis, you didn't lose momentum; you outgrew your mindset." You've been running a powerhouse business based on beliefs that belonged to a past version of you, and it shows in your content, conversions, and energy.

This isn't about fixing anything; it's about remembering who you truly are and rewriting every belief that told you to be smaller, softer, or safer. You don't need more strategy; you need a mindset that aligns with the room you're meant to lead.

Here are some identity statements to help you step into your new leadership style:

- "I no longer believe I have to overdeliver to be successful. Instead, I choose to lead with boundaries and brilliance."
- "I no longer believe I have to tone down my truth to make it palatable. Instead, I choose to lead with clarity and conviction."

At the beginning of my journey in network marketing, I realized I was attracting certain people who just weren't my kind of people. We were on different wavelengths; I was on a different frequency.

Now I have people coming to me who are more aligned with me because they are drawn to my energy, my values, and the way I embody what I teach. It isn't about convincing or closing anymore. It is about connection.

When you're in alignment, you don't attract clients; you attract the right energy. People feel it. They recognize themselves in your story, energy, and integrity. That's when business becomes magnetic, not forced.

Initially, I felt more like a source of inspiration for them, hoping they'd take action to build successful businesses like I had. I think this was because my messaging was influenced by what others were doing, and I was trying to emulate them instead of being true to myself. This approach greatly affected my marketing strategy.

However, a few months later, I shifted my focus. I began to connect more deeply with my true self, recognizing that I have always been a connector and a community builder. While I often hesitate to use the term "recruiter," I genuinely enjoy bringing people together.

As I reflected on my background and what I had been known for since middle school and throughout high school and college, I felt a strong alignment with this authentic self. I realized that building an aligned audience would attract people who resonated with my values and approach. These individuals operated with integrity and were genuinely committed to achieving success while also being willing to take action.

I loved that my clients weren't just hiring me; they were deeply aligned with my morals, values, and mission. My role transformed from simply inspiring them to being a catalyst for inspiration aligned with action. It's challenging to work with a client who invests a significant amount of money but doesn't take any steps forward. It's not merely about the financial transaction; it's about ensuring client success. When my clients succeed, everyone benefits, including me as their coach and mentor. Their success translates to testimonials and a rewarding sense of achievement for me.

When I launched my mastermind program, I became clear about the type of person I wanted to attract. I aimed for six- or seven-figure earners, people who were ready to take action and willing to put in the work. They might have dabbled in online business but lacked a solid understanding of it, and they were eager to learn, saying, "Tell me what to do, and I'll do it."

This shift made me feel much more in alignment with my business methods and direction.

Sometimes, I encounter prospective clients who aren't aligned with me and my mission. When this happens, I typically refer them to someone who might be a better fit for their needs. Alternatively, I have other programs and products that may serve as a better starting point for them.

However, if they want to work with an old version of me or an old way of doing things, I've learned to meet those moments with grace and truth. There was a time when I would've bent, tried to make it work, or gone back to an older version of me just to be chosen, but not anymore. I have realized it's not my job to convince them to come with me; it's to stay anchored in my mission, vision, and evolution.

Every time I choose to honor where I am now, I make space for the clients who are meant to meet me here.

My mastermind and coaching programs are higher-tier and come with a higher price tag. To determine if clients are a good fit, I ask them to fill out an application form. This helps me assess their current mental and financial state, as well as ask the right questions. If I find that the program isn't right for them, I will either suggest a different resource or recommend one of my beginner products instead.

Chapter Summary: Key Takeaways

- Money and success do not eliminate mindset challenges. **Entitlement, power, and external validation** can quietly erode clarity if identity and purpose are not continually recalibrated.
- High-achieving women often wear a polished mask. Even with accolades, income, and support, many feel **exhausted, stuck, and afraid to admit they have outgrown their current identity**.
- Mindset work does not disappear at higher levels. In elite environments, the myth that "I shouldn't be dealing with this anymore" prevents women from addressing **internal misalignment**.
- Burnout at the top often stems from **running an expanded business with outdated beliefs**, such as the need to overdeliver, avoid rest, or prove worth through performance.

- Strategy is rarely the true problem. Most plateaus are caused by an **identity lag**, where growth outpaces mindset, leading to self-editing, shrinking, and hesitation despite credibility.
- Motivation can fuel momentum temporarily, but only **mindset recalibration** creates sustainability. Recalibration shifts leadership from force to **flow, alignment, and truth**.
- True leadership requires releasing inherited rules and beliefs that no longer apply, including ideas like **success requires sacrifice**, **rest must be earned**, or **visibility demands overperformance**.
- Recalibrating mindset means **reprogramming identity**, not adding more habits. It requires replacing outdated beliefs with new truths that support ease, presence, and authority.
- When identity and frequency align with authority, results shift quickly. **Clarity replaces chasing**, clients respond differently, and opportunities expand without added strategy.
- Sustainable success is built by leading from **self-trust, embodiment, and evolved identity**, not by proving worth or maintaining momentum at the cost of alignment.

CHAPTER 4

ENERGY IS YOUR SALES STRATEGY

Energy is essential in business, and it's important to understand what it truly means and why it matters. Energy is not just a vibe or a way to manifest sales; it's not simply about having good or bad days.

In business, energy serves as your internal GPS. It reflects how aligned you are with what you're selling and how congruent your messaging is with your actions. Your energy encompasses your entire state of being, shaping every result you experience, whether that relates to sales, attracting the right people, or otherwise.

While strategy acts as the vehicle, your energy is the driver. I've experienced many instances where, if my personal life feels off, my energy in business shifts as well. This, in turn, affects how I show up, influencing my sales, the people I'm connecting with, and everything I do.

Marketing is also impacted by energy. I know this personally. There was a time when I put out an offer that didn't feel aligned with who I was. Consequently, my energy was off, leading to the offer flopping. I think I only made one sale, if that. This particular offer revolved around Instagram growth strategies, an area where I excel. However, the offer I created wasn't in alignment with what I needed to share to attract the right audience. Internally, I could feel that disconnect.

I genuinely believe that people can sense your energy before they even engage with your content or hear your pitch. Energy is incredibly powerful.

How you present yourself online and in person affects how people perceive you. I've always had a knack for this, even during challenging times. My energy, whether it's showing up with a smile or being ready to socialize, has consistently attracted others to me.

Energy serves as a tool for conversion in every interaction, whether it's through direct messages, posts, Zoom calls, or in-person encounters. I often refer to it as your heartbeat.

When you're experiencing tough times and your energy feels off, working to shift it can change the entire frequency at which people see you, impacting how your offers sell and how your business grows. There's a significant link between energy and conversion. Energy is highly contagious. If you're dealing with personal issues, that can translate to your business, brand, and client interactions. Transformation is something you cannot deny.

I realized that the hustle and grind I experienced led to burnout, but it was a different kind of hustle. It wasn't an aligned hustle. To achieve better results with less effort, I became radically honest with myself.

I addressed my doubts and focused on improving my mindset. I stopped trying to prove myself and started to genuinely embody this new identity and way of building my business.

The results were incredible: clients came to me out of nowhere, but they weren't just any clients. They were aligned clients, clients who were a reflection of me and whom I could guide from A to Z.

These clients were the ones I could truly help because of the energy shift I was experiencing and my increased online presence. My DMs transformed into deposits. I felt like the messages I received were from people eager to work with me, attracted by my energy.

I was no longer just visible; I was vibrating at a different and more aligned level. This shift made people want to be in my space and join my unique movement in this industry.

Now I want to discuss the difference between showing up and performing, specifically addressing the myth of the "doing trap."

The performance trap involves creating polished content, perfect photos, and carefully curated images. While it's possible to produce such content, if there's no soul behind it and it lacks alignment, it falls flat. It simply won't convert; instead, it will feel disconnected, and people will sense it.

When someone is showing up by following the formula but their DMs are dry and sales are stalling, it's often a matter of performance rather than presence. If your content is polished but lacks connection, people can tell. They might like or comment, but they won't convert.

Why is that? It's because you're performing for approval rather than showing up in alignment. You might be selling what looks good instead of what feels authentic, which is the real repellent.

Many high achievers become caught in a "doing loop," thinking that more tasks, more content, and more strategies are the answer. This mindset can lead to burnout or even make someone want to quit altogether. When your energy is not clean, the results don't resonate, and you can't fake congruence. Your audience senses it when your strategy is merely compensating for a lack of alignment.

Operating from a place of depletion can lead to client resentment. This is a significant red flag because relationships are your revenue. Sales calls might become draining or unexciting. Offers can cease to convert, and your brand might appear vibrant but feel empty. I've frequently observed this happening.

True energetic alignment isn't about "doing it right." Instead, it's deeply rooted in believing in what you're selling. It involves being emotionally connected to your mission and vision, and your content should feel like a conversation, not a campaign.

This is essential: energetic alignment is about being grounded. When you believe in your offer, you are connected to your mission. You are not just selling; you are sharing something you know can transform lives. When you're aligned, your message holds true depth, your posture reflects certainty, and your brand becomes a portal, not merely a pitch.

Here's why your audience feels you before they trust you. People, especially those with means, are incredibly intuitive. They can sense when something is off. They can feel it when you're second-guessing yourself or forcing confidence rather than owning it. This is why copying others doesn't lead to conversions when your energy is misaligned. It's not the offer; it's the energy behind it.

It's not about the platform; it's about the presence behind the message. You don't need to be perfect. What you need is to be fully present, honest, and powerful. That's the embodiment advantage.

I want to introduce the idea of energetic embodiment as a sales superpower. Embodiment means alignment between beliefs, brand, and behavior. When someone embodies her message, everything becomes magnetic.

Embodiment is your edge. It occurs when your beliefs, brand, and behavior are in perfect sync. You can't help but talk about what you believe in because it feels natural and energetic. You're no longer just saying the right thing; you're living it.

You're not seeking validation or trying to prove anything. Instead, you become living evidence of your offer.

When a woman embodies her truth, her words resonate more deeply. Her presence commands attention, and her brand becomes undeniable. Embodiment transforms her message from mere content into conversion energy, and that's powerful.

Energy plays a crucial role in sales, content creation, and leadership. Energy shifts can lead to specific outcomes. For example, in sales, a person closes more deals when she energetically leads the room.

If you want to increase your sales, step into that leadership role with energy, excitement, and authenticity. Energy is contagious; it attracts and converts.

The same principle applies to content. Posts resonate more when written from a place of conviction and truth. Additionally, as a leader, your team will reflect your energetic patterns, whether positive or negative.

Let me share a story about one of my clients, Ashley. She had everything: a polished brand, beautiful funnels, and a content team generating strategies daily. Despite this, her sales were inconsistent, and her messages weren't landing. She began to question everything.

What changed? We paused her launch and stripped away the noise. She reconnected with her authentic voice rather than the filtered version of herself. We delved deeply into who she was and who she had always been, grounding her messaging in a way that attracted the version of her past self in need of her products and offers.

Ashley stopped relying on strategy and began sharing more of her true self and what genuinely mattered to her, rather than what others thought. Within two weeks, she received an influx of direct messages. During a masterclass she hosted, a hundred people signed up, and sales started pouring in before she even discussed her offers. Attendees were already in the chat, asking for details.

Her audience felt her energy and responded with cash, not just clicks. People wanted to engage with her because of this authenticity. She didn't need better tactics; she needed true alignment and to reconnect with why she started her business in the first place.

Here are some prompts to help you reflect on your energetic presence:

1. Do I believe in this offer, or am I trying to convince myself?
2. What energy do I bring to my content?
3. Where am I leaking energy in my business, through over-giving, second-guessing, or resentment?
4. When was the last time I showed up fully, not just for a launch but for myself?
5. When was the last time I felt energized by my business, rather than simply feeling responsible for it?
6. Where am I operating out of obligation instead of overflow?
7. What am I offering that no longer excites me?
8. What would I change if my energy led the room, rather than just my expertise?

This version of you, the one who doesn't perform, is the one that people want to buy from. These aren't just cute journaling prompts; they're your personal frequency check. Energy isn't something you can fake; it's something you own.

Frequency equals filtering. The wrong clients can't feel your energy when you're anchored, and that's a good thing.

Your frequency repels misalignment and attracts readiness. When your energy is anchored in truth, something powerful happens: you stop attracting clients who drain you, stop convincing people to buy, and start commanding attention.

Your frequency becomes your filter. The wrong clients won't even sense you, and that's a gift because you're not here to be available to everyone.

When you try to talk to everyone, you end up talking to no one. You're here to activate those who are ready, those who are drawn to your space. If your energy is clear, bold, and aligned, the right people will find you, and they'll find you quickly.

This is an energy movement that truly transforms your business success and the success of your potential clients as well. It's about frequency over force.

I want to discuss the fear of being too much or too authentic and how it can limit your sales. When you dilute your true self, you confuse your audience. However, when you fully embrace your boldness, the right customers will buy without hesitation.

As a coach who has worked with powerful women hiding in plain sight, I've observed this: you're not afraid of failure; you're afraid of being fully seen. Being seen often leads to being misunderstood.

Many opt to play it safe to remain accepted, but in doing so, they water down the very essence that could drive conversions.

Let me be clear: When you dilute yourself, you confuse your audience. However, when you embody your boldest truth, the right people will buy without any hesitation.

Your edge isn't a risk; it's your truth in motion.

Here's a framework I teach called the Energetic Funnel. It's a straightforward method for aligning your energy with sales.

The model consists of four key components:

1. Internal Belief: Do you genuinely believe in what you're selling? This is a crucial question to ask yourself because it truly matters. If you don't believe in your product, how can you expect anyone else to?
2. Embody Messaging: Are you communicating from a place of lived experience rather than using templated phrases? Authenticity is vital in your messaging.
3. Energetic Transmission: Do your words resonate with your true self? It's essential that your message feels authentic to you.
4. Magnetic Conversion: Are you attracting the right clients, or are you trying to appeal to everyone? Remember, when you attempt to speak to everyone, you ultimately reach no one. It's crucial to be clear about who you want to attract, your ideal client.

This isn't just mindset fluff; this is a new sales strategy for women who have moved beyond outdated sales techniques. This is the recalibrated model.

Aligning Energy to Sales

When energy leads, you stop chasing.

You cease over-explaining. You stop marketing out of fear, pressure, or scarcity. Instead, you become a mirror for the woman who is already searching for you.

She doesn't need another tip; she needs to feel you and think, *That's it! That's what I've been missing.*

I want to share a personal shift I experienced when I stopped marketing for conversions and began showing up with conviction. This shift is something I'll never forget. I moved away from launching with performance energy.

I stopped posting with the mindset that *I hope this hits.* I let go of the strategies that looked good on paper and leaned into what actually felt right. And what happened?

Clients began coming in at a higher price point. Sales felt sacred instead of draining. My message no longer needed hype; it carried weight. I became magnetic because I finally gave myself permission to show up as my true self, rather than as a version I thought others wanted me to be.

I attracted clients who weren't my ideal fit. Though I felt I could help them, I was already in a different phase of my coaching journey. I wanted to work with high-achieving women who knew who they were, those who might have had six- or seven-figure businesses but didn't know how to build a presence online.

When I shifted my messaging around what I was offering in my marketing plan, I began attracting clients who were excited and eager to invest. They were the ones ready to pay at a high tier. Interestingly, I even raised the price of my last offer and ended up attracting more aligned clientele than ever before.

This shift occurred when I finally gave myself permission to show up authentically, be true to myself, and align with my offers and products. The work felt exciting again, as I was no longer operating from a place of comparison or trying to emulate someone else's success.

I realized that maintaining energy and boundaries is essential. I believe that energy is protected not just by resting but also through ruthless clarity. Often, women feel exhausted not because they are busy, but because they are boundless. Every leak, whether it's undercharging or saying yes to too much, costs them energetically and financially.

I see this a lot in our community: There's a movement of women striving to "thrive," but many are doing it because it's the trend, not because it's truly aligned with who they're called to become. This can lead to feelings of exhaustion and depletion because they're acting for others rather than themselves.

Protecting your energy means doing so while feeling rested, not resting to the point of inaction, but resting with purpose. So, let's scratch that and focus on how you can reclaim aligned energy. This encompasses your standards, voice, and commanding presence.

Are you currently setting standards and boundaries that will help you attract the people you truly want to work with? Is your voice coming from a place of confidence and certainty about who you are and what you want to share with the world? When you're in the room, does your presence command attention so that people are ready to listen, engage, and take action?

Your clients will rise or fall to your level of embodiment. Energy isn't just a nice addition; it's fundamental, the essence that defines your brand within the broader context. It's crucial to present your brand in a way that attracts people and keeps them engaged for the long term.

This doesn't mean doing more; it means coming back to your center because your energy is a conversion strategy. Your team can schedule content, and your VA can handle the backend, but only you can infuse your brand with the frequency it requires.

So, here's your challenge: I invite you to complete these statements and embrace these affirmations:

- "The version of me who attracts easeful sales is ______."
- "When I fully believe in ________, I become magnetic."
- "I'm no longer marketing for likes. I'm marketing from alignment."

- "I release the need to hustle for what aligned energy will magnetize."
- "I trust my frequency more than any funnel."

I believe my childhood trauma made me long for a sense of love and worth. I think many people feel this way, but I didn't grow up in a safe environment; it was quite toxic.

When I finally reached an age where I could work, I found myself collecting people's contact information, whether phone numbers or pager numbers. I wanted to stay connected with others and share personal stories with them to foster vulnerability and build relationships. This was important to me because I didn't experience that safety growing up. Collecting business cards and reaching out to people felt like a natural instinct; I wasn't consciously connecting it to my trauma at the time.

Later on, I realized that my desire to connect stemmed from a deep-seated need to feel seen and valued, something I lacked as a child. I wanted to create a safe space that was different from my experiences growing up, where I wouldn't just assume I'd never see someone again.

Living in a tourist city while bartending meant that I interacted with many transient people. I recall a moment in Tampa when I met a guy and exchanged business cards with him. Later, after moving to San Diego, he unexpectedly recognized me at a bar where I was working. He remembered me because of the email I had sent him back in Tampa.

These kinds of connections happen to me frequently. I'm always networking and building genuine relationships because I believe they're a vital source of revenue. Whether it's for a business opportunity or a personal recommendation for services like a dentist or a doctor, these connections have been fundamental to my identity and the success of multiple businesses I've built, including my current venture. I feel that genuine relationships are becoming increasingly rare.

I value relationships a lot. I now understand that my childhood and family dynamics weren't safe or focused on building strong relationships. I wanted to create something different for myself and feel seen and valued. I recognized that if I wanted to create that, others probably did too. This understanding has shaped the way I approach my entire life.

Yes, it's definitely a thing, but I didn't initially notice it. As someone with a Type A personality, driven and focused on building businesses, I've experienced a lot of success. However, that drive often comes with a hustle mentality. The problem arises when I reach burnout, which I have encountered multiple times across all my businesses.

In the beginning, there's a thrill of excitement that's hard to control. I am captivated by the shiny new idea of building and creating something as a legacy. However, if my efforts aren't aligned, whether after a month, several months, or some other timeframe, that's when burnout can occur.

I see a back-and-forth dynamic between hustle and alignment. The hustle often feels like an attempt to chase transactions or check items off my to-do list. The question becomes: am I truly in alignment, where there's no checklist and success happens organically, rather than being driven by financial gain?

It was difficult for me to recognize this distinction at first, but over time, I've become more aware of the shifts between hustle and alignment. It can be a challenge, but acknowledging both aspects has helped me navigate this journey more effectively.

Chapter Summary: Key Takeaways

- **Energy is essential in business**. It is not just a vibe or manifestation tool. It functions as your **internal GPS**, revealing how aligned you are with what you sell and how congruent your message is with your actions.
- **Strategy is the vehicle, but energy is the driver**. When your personal life feels off, or your offer is misaligned, your energy shifts, and the ripple effect shows up in **sales, visibility, and client attraction**.
- People can often **sense your energy before they engage**. This is why an offer can flop even when the strategy is solid, because the audience feels the **disconnect behind the message**.
- The chapter exposes the **performance trap**. Polished content without soul becomes empty. When you follow formulas for approval instead of showing up with presence, content may get engagement, but it will not **convert**.
- The **doing loop** creates burnout. More content, more tasks, and more strategy cannot compensate for **unclean energy** or lack of alignment, and over time, it can lead to **resentment, depletion, and stalled growth**.
- **Energetic alignment** is a grounded belief in your offer. When you know what you sell transforms lives, your posture becomes certain, your message gains depth, and your brand becomes a **portal, not a pitch**.
- **Embodiment is a sales superpower**. When beliefs, brand, and behavior are in sync, your presence becomes magnetic and your message shifts from information to **conversion energy**.

- **Frequency becomes your filter**. When you are anchored, you stop attracting clients who drain you, stop convincing people to buy, and start drawing in those who are ready and aligned.
- Diluting yourself confuses your audience. When you embrace your boldness and truth, the right clients buy with clarity because your edge becomes **truth in motion**.
- The chapter introduces the **Energetic Funnel** framework: **Internal Belief, Embodied Messaging, Energetic Transmission, and Magnetic Conversion**. When energy leads, you stop chasing, boundaries strengthen, and sales feel **sacred instead of draining**.

CHAPTER 5

THE AUTHORITY GAP

Visibility Does Not Equal Authority

Your messaging must align with your audience. To effectively connect, you need to know who you're speaking to. If you're trying to speak to everyone, you end up speaking to no one. The key is to share your story clearly.

For instance, I had a personal Instagram account for my previous business. A few years ago, I created a new Instagram account, and I noticed a significant difference in my messaging between the two.

On my old account, my messaging wasn't attracting my ideal clients or building my business in an aligned way. While it was building the business, it felt more transactional. At that time, I wasn't paying close attention to it.

In contrast, my current account conveys the image of someone who knows what she's doing, an authority figure, and a leader. My audience respects me, and my messaging effectively attracts my dream clients, those who are ready to take action. I'm now seen as an authority rather than just a lifestyle figure sharing fun experiences and travels.

While you can still incorporate fun and travel into your content, the messaging and overall presentation must evolve. This change has been incredibly beneficial in how I communicate and connect with my audience, leading to a more aligned business.

Many professional women confuse visibility with credibility. I often see women who are polished and professional yet still feel invisible. The reality is that visibility without authority is merely performance, and performance alone doesn't pay.

Such a woman may be in the room but not taking the mic; she might be online but not top of mind. Despite working harder and showing up more vibrantly, she still gets overlooked for bigger opportunities that she is qualified for. Just because someone is visible does not mean they are credible enough for someone to want to work with them.

When you are highly active but underleveraged, it feels disheartening. People may see you everywhere, yet they don't truly understand what you do. They might feel inspired, but they aren't hiring; they're watching, but they aren't investing.

This discrepancy often arises because, although your presence is professional, your positioning is passive. The most painful realization can be that people still perceive you as someone you have already outgrown.

I remember a time when I was visible but underestimated. I was launching my offers, delivering results, and building a powerful and successful business, yet I watched less-experienced women command the spotlight. They weren't better than I was; they simply owned their expertise and communicated it louder than I did. I positioned myself as the coach, but I wasn't seen as the category leader.

The shift I made didn't come from a rebrand; it came from a reintroduction. I decided to embody the version of myself that my next-level client needed. I allowed my content, tone, and offers to reflect that evolution clearly and unapologetically.

Perception is a real issue. It highlights the concept of the authority gap: the professional woman may be known, but she is not revered. She's visible but not respected at her true level. This is what we call the authority gap. It occurs when your audience is still applauding your past but hasn't acknowledged your present brilliance.

Until the perception shifts, the world continues to refer to you by your old name. This is how high-level women often outgrow their reputations. They build brands that once worked for them.

Perhaps the woman was known as the branding expert, the systems coach, the founder, or the healer, but now she is something more: more embodied, more involved, and more expansive than the label she's still answering to. The market doesn't recognize this because she hasn't claimed her true value.

People don't pay her what she's worth, not because she isn't worth it, but because she hasn't reintroduced her value clearly. This isn't about her worthiness for premium rates; it's about her positioning not effectively communicating that worth. When people still associate you with your past branding, they don't realize they're underpaying you. They believe they are paying the right price for the wrong level of expertise.

This is precisely why the high-level woman often gets overlooked for higher-end clients, $25,000 contracts, and invitations to speak on powerful stages. It's not that she isn't ready; it's that her brand hasn't signaled that she is. Although she has pivoted internally, she is still showing up as the person she no longer is.

Her strategy might be elevated, and her identity might be embodied, but her brand hasn't caught up. She's attracting beginner-level clients because she is still broadcasting a beginner-level message. This disconnect is what keeps high-level women trapped in low-level cycles.

I want to share how I helped a client reframe this problem. It's not about getting louder; it's about becoming clearer, bolder, and more aligned with her new identity.

When clients come to me feeling stuck, they often say, "I don't understand. I'm doing all the things. Why isn't it working?" My answer is simple: It's not about getting louder. It's about getting clearer, more precise, more embodied, and more aligned with who you are now, not who you were when you built your first six figures. Once we achieve this clarity, the brand stops whispering and starts converting.

Perception Audit Prompts

I invite you to reflect on some high-level perception questions:

- What assumptions do people still hold about me that are no longer true?
- What do I want to be known for that I haven't declared yet?
- In what areas have I grown, but my online presence hasn't kept pace?
- What labels have I accepted for the sake of comfort, even though I have outgrown them?

This exercise is not about rebranding; it's about reclaiming your voice and repositioning yourself as an authority.

One of my clients came to me with impressive results: a six-figure business and years of behind-the-scenes leadership experience. However, her message still reflected the early days of her Instagram journey. It wasn't her offer that caused people to underestimate her; it was how she was perceived.

We worked together to reframe the way she communicated her brilliance. We elevated her tone, clarified her promise, and made sure her current identity was reflected across all aspects of her brand: offers, visuals, content, positioning, and marketing. She transformed from being seen as simply helpful to becoming undeniably valuable.

Her voice became more confident, and her posture grew more authoritative. Instead of receiving messages like *"Can I pick your brain?"* her DMs shifted to *"How can I pay you?"* Her content didn't change in frequency; she did. She moved from being visible to being respected.

I teach a framework for this transformation. It involves moving from visible to respected by aligning three key elements:

1. Message: What you say.
2. Position: What you own.
3. Perception: How others feel about you.

If any of these elements are misaligned, even the most brilliant women can be overlooked. It's essential to ensure that your message is clear, you position yourself as a leader or authority, and you create a positive perception when you're present. Gaps in any of these areas can create friction. When message, position, and perception align, trust is built more quickly.

With alignment, premium pricing feels natural, and high-caliber clients actively seek you out. Conversely, when they are misaligned, you end up working twice as hard for half the impact.

However, many high-achieving women evolve behind the scenes but fail to announce this evolution to the public. They may have outgrown their old brand but continue to post with the same tone, visuals, and tired talking points. They have already become the best version of themselves in private; now it's time to introduce this new identity to the world.

My public reintroduction created a ripple effect when I started being more visible. The day I stopped presenting myself merely as a coach and began speaking as a category leader, everything changed. People started approaching me differently, paying me differently, and quoting me differently.

This shift didn't occur because I changed my offers; it happened because I stopped downplaying my authority. I remember that moment clearly, as I initially felt self-doubt and uncertainty about altering how I was perceived online. After all, I'm human. However, once I embraced this change, it significantly impacted my offers and pricing. I felt more aligned and developed a stronger, more authoritative tone in how I presented myself.

If your calendar is full but your soul feels frustrated, if you're working harder than your title reflects, or if you know you've outgrown how the world sees you, this is your cue. Your business doesn't need more effort; it needs a reintroduction to your evolution.

So, I challenge you with this prompt: If the next level of my business depended on how clearly I communicate who I am, what would I say differently, starting now?

Say it, post it, own it, and let the world catch up to who you've already become.

Looking back, I realize that I was just posting and hoping for the best. I was trying to figure out my identity, my messaging, and how people would perceive me.

That's when I realized the shift had already happened. I was no longer performing for approval or shrinking the parts of me that felt too soft, too real, too much. For the first time, I chose to be seen for who I actually am, not the version that survived, but the one that is finally living.

As I became increasingly uncomfortable and engaged in activities I wasn't sure would succeed or fail, I knew I was becoming more aligned with who I really was.

I felt a significant shift in March 2024, and everything began to take off. It felt like I had cracked a code. I discovered my brand and what I stand for. Although I still have moments of shifting and exploring certain aspects, for the most part, what I do feels true to me.

The whole concept of alignment, building an audience that resonates with my values, and being true to myself is at the core of my brand. It's about being in tune with what my soul craves and who I am as a person.

There are several questions that can help explore this topic. Generally speaking, whether in business or personal life, we all experience different identity shifts. A lot of this can be influenced by our peers and the communities we engage with. When I work with clients undergoing such changes, I like to ask them about their current personal situation, who their peers are, and the support they are receiving, as these factors can significantly impact their journey.

I would tell someone who wants to reintroduce themselves, "You don't need to know who you are yet; you just have to be willing to stop pretending to be who you aren't. The 'you' that you have been searching for isn't lost; she's just buried under expectations, survival, and old stories. Give yourself permission to slow down, get curious, and meet her again without the pressure to perform, just the desire to be real."

This influence can be substantial. During a period of rebirth or identity transformation, it's essential for the person to accept that their old version may linger, but that they are now stepping into a higher frequency that will attract a different kind of person aligned with their current state.

I see this frequently, but my clients often struggle with fear and doubt, which can surface during this process. It comes down to shifting their mindset and granting them permission to let go of their old identity and embrace a new one. Sometimes, that's all they need: permission to release the past and step into something new that feels real and aligned.

When they do this, it's as if their soul is ready to leap into the world, and they feel an overwhelming urge to express themselves.

I believe this desire to be seen and valued stems from a common need for love and recognition. Going back to my earlier point about caring what others think, I think everyone wants to feel loved, important, and acknowledged. This is really the crux of the matter.

Many people, perhaps due to their upbringing, experienced a lack of recognition from their parents for their accomplishments, whether big or small. As a result, they may come from a place of wanting to be noticed. It's not about ego; it's more about a genuine desire to know that they are doing good in the world.

Ultimately, we all want to feel that we matter, that we are loved, and that we are seen. Fulfilling this universal need can truly nourish a person's heart and soul.

Chapter Summary: Key Takeaways

- **Visibility does not equal authority**. Being seen everywhere does not automatically translate to being trusted, respected, or hired at your true level.
- When your **messaging is unclear or too broad**, you end up speaking to everyone and resonating with no one. Authority requires knowing exactly who you are speaking to and why.
- Many professional women confuse **polish with credibility**. Visibility without authority becomes performance, and performance alone does not convert or sustain growth.
- The **authority gap** occurs when your audience applauds a past version of you while overlooking your present

brilliance. You are known, but not yet revered at your current level.

- Being underpaid or overlooked for high-level opportunities is often a **positioning issue**, not a worthiness issue. People pay based on perception, not potential.
- Growth requires **reintroduction, not rebranding**. As you evolve internally, your content, tone, offers, and positioning must clearly reflect who you are now.
- High-level women often attract beginner-level clients because their brand is still broadcasting a **beginner-level message**, even when their expertise has expanded.
- Authority is built when the **message, position, and perception align**. When these elements are congruent, trust accelerates and premium opportunities feel natural.
- Becoming respected does not require getting louder. It requires becoming **clearer, bolder, and more embodied** in how you communicate your value.
- Your next level does not require more effort. It requires **owning your evolution**, declaring who you are now, and allowing the world to catch up to the woman you have already become.

CHAPTER 6

THE BRAND THAT SPEAKS BOLDLY WHEN IT NO LONGER FITS

Imagine a professional woman who has built a bold offer and created real results. Her income proves she's experienced, yet her brand still resembles a side hustle.

Her visuals are outdated, soft, or safe. Although her voice is powerful, her posts feel flat. She possesses high confidence, but her positioning is still timid.

She recognizes that she has evolved, but her audience continues to view her through the lens of who she used to be.

I want to discuss the energetic misalignment between her current power and her positioning. She has become louder in the wrong ways, producing more content and posting more frequently, while becoming quieter in the areas that matter most.

Her core messaging, pricing, and positioning reflect a disconnect. There is power within her, but her brand does not showcase it. It isn't that she needs a complete rebrand; rather, her external expression hasn't caught up with her internal growth.

I want to share a personal story.

I recall the moment clearly. My offers were high-caliber, and my coaching was next-level, yet the market still treated me as merely a content coach. This misunderstanding wasn't the audience's fault; it was mine for not updating the mirror I was holding up.

The moment I clarified my voice, owned my tone, and stopped filtering for approval, my pricing shifted, my audience matured, and I transitioned from being watched to being pursued. It wasn't about aesthetics; it was all about alignment.

Your brand is speaking; what is it saying?

Even when you're not posting or during quiet periods between launches, silence conveys a message. Inconsistency sends a signal. Playing it safe is still a form of branding, just not the one she desires. You don't get to choose whether your brand speaks; you only get to choose what it says.

The high-achieving woman doesn't need a rebrand; she needs a reintroduction. She has evolved and expanded but still feels the need to explain herself to an audience she has outgrown.

It's not about new color palettes or bios; it's about owning her current identity openly. She doesn't need permission to stop over-explaining and start embodying.

Let's discuss her brand, which has already secured a strong "yes" before the sales call even begins. High-ticket clients don't buy from confusion; they buy from certainty. Before she even gets on a sales call, her brand has already made a statement. Is she the one? Is she embodied? Is she leading from depth rather than noise? Branding isn't just about appearance; it's the pre-sale. When it speaks boldly, she doesn't pitch; she invites.

Here's a framework I like: embodied branding.

Embodied branding equals message plus identity plus delivery. The message is what she articulates and why it matters. The identity is who she is when she states it, and the delivery is how that energy is communicated visually, vocally, and emotionally. If any of these elements are off, the brand feels flat, regardless of how strategic it is.

Bold branding doesn't scream; it signals.

Here are some prompts for reflection:

- What part of me is still shrinking within my brand?
- What would my brand say if I stopped filtering?
- What would I say if I didn't need likes to feel legitimate?
- Am I building a brand for approval or for authority?

I want to share the story of one of my clients, Emily. When she came to me, she was already making six figures and coaching elite clients, yet she still had a brand voice that whispered. Her presence felt safe, passive, and pretty. Because of that, she was being underpaid and underestimated.

Once we delved deeper, we discovered the voice she'd been silencing. We aligned her message with her mission, cut the fluff, and clarified her frequency. As a result, her pricing, clients, and confidence all elevated instantly. She started to feel seen. She stopped explaining herself and began stepping into rooms not just as a coach but as a leader. That shift not only increased her income; it also expanded her leadership.

Bold doesn't mean loud. Bold branding is not about being aggressive, flashy, or too much.

For women at this level, being bold often means being honest. It means stating what's true and living that truth, even if it's calm, graceful, and elegantly disruptive. Authenticity often speaks louder than volume.

The most magnetic brands aren't the loudest; they are the clearest. You don't need more glitter; you need more alignment. High-caliber clients don't need hype; they need truth. In the end, the most authentic woman in the room wins.

Emily let go of over-explaining her expertise, speaking to clients she had already outgrown, and playing it safe in the name of being relatable. She reclaimed her identity as a leader, not just a service provider, her values of truth, clarity, and excellence, and her right to charge boldly while speaking directly. Now her brand feels more like home to her. It reflects who she truly is and filters out who she's not.

That's the power of branding from embodiment, not from ego. You don't need another Canva template. You need to stop performing for the room.

You need to stop performing for the room and start owning your seat at the table. If your brand doesn't reflect your brilliance, it's not a problem of strategy; it's a power leak. The woman you've become is waiting to be seen.

I challenge you to declare:

"The version of me who leads my movement no longer apologizes for ____________________.

My brand used to be ________________, but now it's becoming ________________________."

Instead of simply saying, "I help moms lose seven pounds," now say, "I help busy moms who homeschool their kids lose seven pounds." This shift in messaging is crucial.

Your identity is also important; it reflects who you are when you deliver this message. It's essential to be clear about the brand you want to represent, including who you are and what you stand for. This clarity contributes to establishing authority in your space or industry.

Regarding delivery, I understand your perspective. I'm often thinking about businesses and how I can assist them with their mission statements or slogans.

I had two clients, Lakeisha and Maggie, who were taking a course together, and they did a phenomenal job of branding themselves as a duo. They faced some challenges because they were different people with distinct audiences.

We worked together to combine their offers into something that felt aligned for both of them. It was an exciting process! We focused on their color palettes, the elegance of their outfits for pictures, and the messaging that highlighted why their brand mattered. I explained to them that their messaging needed to change because they were attracting a lot of clients who were financially struggling. I helped them understand that they could attract clients willing to pay for their services by establishing their authority and refining their messaging and identity.

Their branding collaboration was incredibly successful; during a seven-day launch, they signed up about thirty people! This success can be attributed to their visual presentation, the colors, elegance, thoughtful messaging, how they defined their identity and what they stood for together. In essence, it was a rebranding effort, but done in a way that showcased their partnership.

Many people don't have a clear understanding of their messaging and identity unless they work with someone who can help them uncover these aspects. This person can guide them in identifying who they stand for and what they want to contribute to the world.

It's easy to get caught up in comparisons; for instance, seeing others who have high engagement, a lot of likes, or are making significant money can be overwhelming.

However, you can often sense that the person being compared to is deeply connected to their truth, their soul, and their God-given purpose. They are in tune with what their soul craves and are focused on their legacy. Sometimes, it simply requires hiring a coach or mentor to draw that out of them. I believe everyone can benefit from having an outsider's perspective, someone to provide insight into what they see and offer suggestions on how to gain authority and secure high-ticket sales.

Everything about you contributes to your brand. This includes your purpose, your skills, how you present yourself, your confidence, your beliefs, and your mission. All of these elements combined define what your brand represents.

When I say that your brand is speaking, I'm referring to what it conveys about you. It's about what you put into the world, which often reflects the saying, "What you put out is what you get back." This concept is very true regarding your brand.

Your brand constantly communicates your truth. I've experienced moments in my life when people recognized me from my Instagram or approached me because of something I shared. For example, when I wear hot pink, a color that signifies my brand, people often assume it's my favorite color, all thanks to the consistency in my messaging and visuals. Even my children associate me with pink because they see me and my belongings presented in that color.

This shows that your brand leaves a lasting impression on others, even without explicit communication. Your brand is essentially you, your truth, how you show up, how you make others feel, and how you look.

I believe that branding is transferable. Your brand is essentially your identity. It reflects who you are and your truth. It can be challenging to convey that online, but once you do, you become recognized for it.

That's your brand. People start to identify you as the person who does a specific thing. For example, before I transitioned to focus on helping people build an aligned audience using the Aligned Audience Method, I primarily posted a lot of Canva hacks and trendy content just to gain followers, engagement, and likes. However, this didn't contribute to building my business or my brand. In fact, I started to be known as the Instagram coach, which was not the image I wanted to project.

While I enjoy teaching Instagram, and it's a part of my mastermind program, I didn't want to be labeled solely as an Instagram coach, especially among so many others in the field. This question is significant because I struggled with it for a long time. Despite being skilled at Instagram, it didn't feel aligned with my true self to merely be another Instagram coach.

I believe that being bold is fundamentally about embracing and expressing your true self and what you offer to the world.

I've worked with clients, especially young women, who embody boldness, but they choose more subtle branding colors. Despite their understated approach, you can sense their authenticity. It creates a feeling of trust; you think, *I like her. She is honest and genuine.*

They bring value without being flashy or aggressive. Their boldness comes from their tone, truthfulness, and honesty. To me, that is the essence of being bold.

Chapter Summary: Key Takeaways

- A woman can have **real results and a high income** while still carrying a brand that feels like a **side hustle**, creating a gap between her true power and how she is perceived.
- When internal growth outpaces external expression, **energetic misalignment** appears. Posting more or getting louder does not fix this; clarity, ownership, and embodiment do.
- The issue is rarely strategy or aesthetics. Most high-achieving women do not need a rebrand; they need a **reintroduction** that reflects who they have become.

- Your brand is always speaking, even in silence. **Playing it safe, inconsistency, and over-filtering** all communicate messages, often ones that undervalue your authority.
- High-ticket clients buy from **certainty, not confusion**. Branding functions as the pre-sale, signaling depth, leadership, and trust before a sales call ever begins.
- **Embodied branding** requires alignment between message, identity, and delivery. When any of these are off, the brand feels flat, no matter how strategic it looks.
- Bold branding is not about being loud or flashy. For women at this level, bold often means **being honest, precise, and unapologetically clear**.
- When a woman stops performing for approval and starts owning her seat at the table, her brand shifts from being watched to being pursued. **Authority follows embodiment**, not effort.

CHAPTER 7

MAGNETIC MESSAGING THAT CONVERTS

When a professional woman's messaging doesn't resonate, it's often due to the disconnect between what she feels she should be doing to get it right and the actual impact her actions are having. She finds herself overwhelmed by a desire to share this knowledge effectively.

She shows up daily in her Instagram stories, on social media, during her webinars, and through long-form content. Everything seems well-organized, yet there is a persistent silence. Although she knows her brilliance, her messaging feels like a remix of every other coach or entrepreneur in her space.

Not only does she feel unseen, but she's also becoming uninspired, a dangerous place for someone who prides herself on excellence. Unlike others who chase metrics, she pursues meaning, yet her message no longer fulfills that desire.

Effective messaging is about aligning with who she truly is and the type of message she wants to share, which will attract her dream clients. Marketing burnout isn't about the amount of effort; it's about emotional disconnection.

She feels exhausted, not due to her workload or how filtered she appears, but because she finds herself hiding behind frameworks and polished language instead of using her authentic voice. It's not the volume of her work that drains her; it's the disconnect between her message and her true self. She's writing what sounds good, what converts, and what aligns with her brand, but none of it genuinely feels like her. She is attempting to come across as "right" instead of "real." Being filtered leaves her feeling powerless; it feels like she's performing rather than being herself.

I remember a time when my own messaging wasn't converting, not because it was bad, but because it lacked boldness. Though it looked flawless, I didn't resonate with my target audience. I garnered likes and comments, but the clients didn't come. I didn't lack strategy; I lacked authenticity in expressing who I was and what I wanted to convey.

To change that, I examined my content to see where I was merely performing or mimicking other coaches rather than staying true to myself. My turning point came when I stopped over-explaining my offers and began naming the unspoken truths my ideal client was already thinking but felt too vulnerable to express. That post didn't go viral; it provoked a visceral response, attracting more premium leads in twenty-four hours than a month's worth of content ever had.

I focused on building an aligned audience of people who resonated with my offers and learned how to refine my messaging to help them convert. I created a beta program and, with just a simple shift in the wording of my email campaigns, spoke directly to my ideal client's needs. Within the first week, I saw an influx of sign-ups, confirming that my messaging was connecting with people seeking answers to their mission.

People don't buy based on perfect posts. We're not in the business of providing tips; we're in the business of transformation. People don't make purchases because of bullet points; they buy because something resonates with them: a truth, a reflection, or a moment where they think, *She sees me.*

That's when the direct messages come pouring in, and the investment feels inevitable. They aren't looking for more data; they are searching for connection and resonance.

Resonance refers to the power of messaging that addresses both inner conflicts and external results. The strongest messages highlight two key areas: the internal conflict, such as feeling unseen despite having built success, and the external desire, like wanting to create a presence that converts even before making a pitch. When you stop posting what your coach tells you to and start articulating what your clients feel but cannot name, that's when you become truly magnetic.

High-ticket messaging isn't about the "how"; it's about the "who." Don't just sell a process; offer powerful self-permission. Your content should answer the question, "Who do I help my client become?" It's not just about what she does but who she becomes once the work is complete. Instead of marketing to pain points, market to an identity upgrade.

I want to outline a simple framework that can help produce messaging that converts. People don't want something polished; they want permission. When clients express thoughts they've never voiced, they invest in you before even hearing the actual offer.

This formula for content that converts doesn't rely on a sales pitch:

1. Truth: What's the real belief your client is afraid to admit?
2. Tension: What's the cost of staying stuck? What's unsaid but obvious?
3. Transformation: What does the client become when she moves through it?

Magnetic messaging is about closing the gap between what you know and what you say publicly. You don't need a better strategy; you need a bolder voice. When you speak truths that others won't, when you stop hiding behind high-value content, and when you express simple or raw honesty, your message becomes unforgettable.

Messaging Self-Audit

Reflect on these questions:

- Does my content reflect what I deeply believe or what I think clients want to hear?
- What am I afraid to say that might actually set me apart?
- If I stopped trying to sound smart or strategic, what would I say instead?
- Am I still addressing the version of my client that I've outgrown?

Magnetic messaging stems from honesty rather than gimmicks.

I had a client, Ashley, who transformed from filtered to fully booked. She was producing weekly content, had stunning branding, and had systems for everything. However, her messaging wasn't specific to her desired niche. Once we shifted her messaging to reflect her authentic self, her voice deepened, her content resonated, and applications for her services flowed seamlessly to attract her ideal client.

The primary change we made was granting her permission to be truthful. I often see clients who are hesitant to take that next step of proclaiming their messages publicly; they fear failure and worry about others' perceptions. When you make this small shift toward greater truth, the right words will come organically and automatically. This client began marketing from a place of conviction rather than confusion, moving away from hoping her message would resonate.

She started saying, "This is the truth; if it's for you, you'll know." At that moment, she stopped explaining her offer and began embodying it.

Content That Converts Without Overthinking

Posting more tips or hacks doesn't inherently build trust. Sometimes, the statement that attracts your premium client isn't a step-by-step guide; it's a resounding "Hell, yes." You don't need to seek validation anymore; you're there to work with women who already know what they want. This kind of post resonates with high-level women, leading them to wonder, *Where have you been?*

Posts like *"I'm not here to convince you; I'm here to mirror you"* can help you attract your ideal client. When content doesn't go viral, it often still attracts the right clients because it is specific, grounded, and undeniable, like messaging in a mirror.

If your content isn't landing, it may be because you haven't fully embraced your new identity. Your message is only as powerful as the version of you who is writing it. When you second-guess, filter, or perform, your words can carry the energy of doubt. However, when you are fully embodied, clear, and convicted, you can say less and have a greater impact.

Premium buyers aren't scanning your carousel for tips; they are looking for alignment. They don't need fluff; they need a woman who knows who she is. When they sense that confidence, they don't just click; they commit.

Your message isn't soft; it's strategic. There's a significant difference between being liked and being booked. You don't need more captions; you need more clarity, and clarity comes from the truth you're no longer willing to hide.

Here's a challenge prompt for you:

- The boldest thing that I believe I've ever been afraid to say is ______.
- If my ideal client saw one of my posts tomorrow, I want her to know ______.

Say it, post it, and let the world respond to your most authentic voice yet.

It's essential to clarify who you want to help and the specific results you can achieve for them. When my clients go through an identity upgrade, I help them make sure their marketing grows with them. We start by getting clear on who they are speaking to with their messaging and their content so it reflects who they've become, not who they were. It's about speaking from truth, not proving.

First, I emphasize how important it is to tell a story about this new version of them that's growing. Second, we make sure that this energy matches their offer suite and make any changes to match their next level. Third, we make sure their energy and integrity are aligned with their new upgrade. Then I coach them to let go of performance and pressure and to build confidence in what they are doing. Energy is contagious, and when it's aligned, your audience can feel it.

Focus on a specific audience. Instead of saying, "I help moms," you should be more specific, like "I help homeschool moms who are entrepreneurs" or "I help busy moms who are on a budget," depending on who you want to attract.

Next, it's important to define how you can achieve these specific results. A lot of this comes from using your life experiences and the expertise you have, skills that you know you are good at. This process helps bridge your old identity with a new one, which is reflected in your core messaging and brand statement.

Identifying your new identity is crucial. For instance, I often think about how I transitioned from being in network marketing to having my own coaching business. I no longer feel like I'm building someone else's business; I'm truly creating my own brand. This shift is aligned with my values, voice, and lifestyle.

Consider the problems you can solve now compared to those in the past. You need to get clear on this, as change is inevitable. Shifting your message to reflect this new perspective is important. Be specific and highlight your new strengths that can help solve various problems. Focus on understanding factors like the age of your target audience, their life stages, desires, and struggles.

This clarity will help you create content that showcases this new version of yourself and demonstrates your expertise in your new niche, enabling you to teach, guide, or inspire others effectively.

So, who is the version of you that already has what they want? Think about how she thinks, how she speaks, how she dresses, how she sets new boundaries, and how she spends her time. It's essentially what I'm experiencing right now.

It's really interesting because I've gone through a significant shift in my personal life, and it feels like I'm caught between my personal and business identities. This change has forced me to shed an identity I held for eight years in order to become a new version of myself that feels more alive. This transformation is crucial for me to show up authentically for my potential clients and in my business moving forward.

When you go through such transitions, it can be overwhelming. Speaking from experience, I've found myself easily distracted by unexpected changes that were not part of the future I envisioned for myself.

So, how do I realign with my goals, vision, and mission in both my business and personal life during this transition?

Sometimes, it's about taking time to be alone and acknowledging this shift as a natural part of growth, rather than viewing it as a failure. It's essential to see this change as a way to propel you in a better direction.

I try to focus on gratitude and recognize the silver linings that existed in my previous identity. It's important to bring the positive attributes from that identity into this new version of myself. Consider how your habits, your environment, and the people you surround yourself with play a significant role in this process. This approach applies to both personal and business aspects of life.

Just as they say with kids, creating structure and rituals can help anchor a new identity. This could involve writing in a journal, reading the Bible, or establishing a morning routine that aligns you with a sense of calm and purpose. Incorporating affirmations and surrounding yourself with supportive people and environments can also reinforce this identity, especially during challenging times when it might feel like everything else is falling apart. Additionally, it's important to celebrate small victories as evidence that you are already the person you aspire to be.

I like to think of this process as an upgrade. It isn't about becoming someone entirely new; rather, it's about shedding the parts of yourself that no longer fit and fully stepping into the version of you that has been waiting. You may have faced obstacles, walls, or setbacks in your past, but now is the time to embrace and embody your true self.

The issue often stems from our need for external validation, such as social norms, likes, and the instant dopamine fix that social media provides. The biggest difference is the energy behind it. Content that isn't real sounds very robotic or polished. Content that sounds real sounds more honest and messy; it moves people because it comes from experience, not performance. However, when we share from a place of truth, values, integrity, and honesty, it becomes a way to express what we truly believe.

When my relationship began, I believed I had found a partnership and shared vision. We were building a life that looked aligned from the outside: family, future, momentum. I showed up as the woman who knew how to hold it all together. At the time, I didn't yet realize how much of myself I was quietly editing to keep the peace.

During my separation, I questioned whether I should share my experience. It felt vulnerable to speak from the middle of change rather than from the other side. Ultimately, the more I became open and authentic, the more unanticipated conversations and connections I sparked. It allowed me to be real instead of just fitting the mold of a social media influencer. Many women reached out to me, sharing that they were experiencing similar shifts in their lives, acknowledging challenges that are often difficult to admit or discuss.

This experience has given me the opportunity to express myself freely and connect with my audience on a deeper level. Building this trust enables them to see me as someone who could help them.

I've realized that the biggest difference comes from doing the right things without seeking approval. It's about aligning with my heart and being genuine. When I am truly real and connect with my audience, it makes them feel seen. In turn, this authenticity allows me to be seen as well, creating a meaningful connection.

I've noticed that when I post just to check a box, like completing a task to stay consistent, my engagement suffers. However, over the past month, I've been posting more from my heart, and my engagement in stories has doubled, even tripled, because of it.

I think it's possible to go back and forth between these two approaches. I can be quite organized and disciplined, which sometimes leads me to be hard on myself. I often feel that I have to stick to a strict routine and follow a predetermined plan; otherwise, I think I'm doing it wrong.

Recently, I decided to let go of that mindset, and I felt excited to post naturally again. I realized I don't have to be so rigid in my approach. While both structure and spontaneity are important, embracing a more heartfelt, less obligatory approach to posting has reignited my enthusiasm for creating.

As a high-ticket buyer, I've realized that when I invest in higher-priced coaching, it's not just about seeking information; I want a true transformation. So, I often ask myself, *Do I feel understood? Do I trust this person to guide me? Can I see myself in her story?*

Emotion is everything in conversion, especially for women making high-level investments. People don't buy information; they buy identity alignment. They're asking, *Do I feel seen, safe, and inspired in her presence?*

When someone feels you, your conviction, your calm, and your certainty, their emotion builds a lot faster than any funnel could. High-ticket buyers aren't looking for more facts; they're looking for a frequency they can rise into.

When someone purchases a high-ticket offer, they are investing in how they want to feel on the other side: confident, free, secure, and successful. This is so true for all the coaches I've worked with. They have provided more than just information; they have offered a sense of understanding and trust.

Information is abundant; you can find it everywhere, on Google, YouTube, and through free downloads. But buyers aren't paying between $5,000 and $20,000 for facts. They pay for certainty, clarity, and a guide to their desired path.

I believe that if your marketing focuses solely on delivering information and teaching, you risk becoming a free resource rather than a trusted authority figure. How can people trust you as an authority in your space? What sets you apart from everyone else who is offering free information constantly?

The emotional connection is vital. When I see a statement that resonates with me, I think, *That's me. She understands me.* When your words and story reflect the hidden fears and desired futures of your buyers, you cut through the noise. This makes them feel seen, safe, and inspired to take action.

Previously, on my Instagram, I focused more on inspired content, and as a result, my audience didn't feel the same connection. They didn't feel seen, safe, or inspired to act. That's what I truly want because, when my clients succeed, I succeed as well. For me, it's not just a transaction; it's a transformation. When they experience a transformation, something profound happens internally for them.

I believe this is especially important for high-ticket buyers. They are not just looking for the best price; they want to know if they can trust you as they move into the next phase of their journey. They are seeking assurance that you will hold them accountable and guide them through any resistance they may face.

I can't do this alone. In fact, I recently spoke with a fitness coach about starting a new program. I've been involved in health, fitness, and nutrition for a long time, and I know what needs to be done. The information is readily available; there's a ton of it out there. But for me, the real question is whether he will hold me accountable and provide guidance throughout the process.

What I'm truly seeking is confidence. I want someone to walk alongside me, someone I can connect with on a deeper level, someone I can trust.

Chapter Summary: Key Takeaways

- When messaging stops resonating, it is rarely a strategy issue. It is usually the result of a **disconnect between who a woman is becoming and what she feels she should say** to get it right.
- Showing up consistently does not guarantee impact. When messaging feels like a remix of others in the industry, it signals **performance over presence**, leaving the woman unseen and uninspired.
- Marketing burnout is not caused by effort or volume. It is caused by **emotional disconnection**, hiding behind frameworks, polished language, and filtered messaging instead of speaking from truth.
- Messaging converts when it moves from being "right" to being **real**. People do not buy perfect posts or bullet points; they buy resonance, recognition, and the feeling of being deeply seen.
- High-ticket messaging is about **identity, not instruction**. Clients are not buying a process or a how-to; they are buying permission to become the next version of themselves.
- Magnetic messaging names the truths clients are already thinking but are afraid to say. When content addresses both **internal conflict and external desire**, it becomes unforgettable.
- The most powerful content follows a simple framework: **truth, tension, and transformation**. When these are present, conversion happens without selling.
- Premium buyers are not searching for more information. They are searching for **certainty, emotional safety, and alignment** with a woman who knows who she is and leads with conviction.

CHAPTER 8

THE BROKEN-SCALE STRATEGY

Sometimes, scaling starts to feel like shrinking.

The professional woman followed the plan: she built the funnel, hired the team, and automated her offers. Now, though, she feels further from her clients than ever. Her inbox is full, yet her presence is missing. She's making more moves, but they lack meaning.

The heartbreaking part is that she built the business of her dreams, and now it feels like a machine. She traded intimacy for infrastructure, and the very things meant to free her have started to flatten her.

She's scaling like a pro, but she's showing up as a shadow of her former self. Her once bold message is buried within workflows. Her launches feel mechanical; her content, while polished, is lifeless.

She's not burned out from output; she's burned out from the lack of emotional return. She misses the fire, the connection, and the reason why she started. She didn't enter business to become a glorified operations manager.

I remember when I hired my team, plugged them into all the blueprints, and delegated everything because that's what I was advised to do by seasoned CEOs: delegate, delegate. However, no one warned me about the hidden cost. My business kept running, but I no longer felt present in it.

I realized I had followed someone else's version of scaling, one that didn't fit my leadership style and stripped away the essence I had spent years building. So, I rebuilt it, not from scratch but from a place of sovereignty.

At one point, I hired two personal assistants to help build content, images, and marketing. But the more I delegated, the more disconnected I felt. I was the one who created from alignment and heart. When you hire out and delegate, which isn't necessarily bad, it's crucial to find someone aligned with your mission and goals, someone who can embody your vision. Otherwise, there will be a disconnect, and people will feel it through your marketing, emails, content, and even your flyers and images.

Ultimately, I had to let those assistants go. No matter how much I trained them to think like me, it just didn't work. At that moment, I could feel the shift in my business, and not in a positive way. Finding someone who aligns with you is possible, but it wasn't occurring for me at that time.

The real reason scaling stalls is not due to exhaustion from effort; it's from process-driven burnout. The professional woman shows up but doesn't truly plug in. Her clients feel her absence. Her team feels confused. She feels invisible in a business that bears her name. It's not that the systems are broken; they're just running without her unique energy.

There's an illusion of growth metrics versus the reality of stagnant revenue and reach. Her backend is optimized, her workflows are efficient, and her CRM buzzes with leads, but the revenue is stagnant, the reach is flat, and the resonance is missing. The reason for this is that growth without embodiment is merely an illusion.

The biggest leaps in revenue don't come from automations; they come from alignment, as it brings emotional connection with your audience. Scaling should amplify your voice, not replace it.

This woman's voice was the reason people initially bought in. Her energy was the funnel; her presence was the brand. She can delegate many tasks, but her essence, her most scalable asset, lives within her funnel. It's about clarity and conviction.

Here's a framework for scaling with presence.

Systems serve power; they don't replace it. Scaling through presence means creating a structure that amplifies identity rather than erasing it. This distinction separates a leader-led business from a template-led one. In a leader-led business, strategy adapts to the leader's energy, while in a template-led business, energy is often buried under rigid strategies.

Let me explain the concept of presence-led scaling. It involves prioritizing your energy and identity, allowing the system to be tailored to fit who you truly are. Instead of relying on someone else's blueprint or following the methods of a different coach, you design structures that support your natural flow and authenticity.

This approach preserves your inherent power while integrating systems that support scale. With a leader-led strategy, you don't shrink yourself to fit a template. Your presence, vision, and unique strengths lead the way and the systems are built to amplify them.

On the other hand, a template-led approach can bury your energy under rigid strategies, forcing you to adhere to someone else's formula. This can lead to losing your spark, as the system overshadows your identity. I've seen this happen frequently in the industry, and I've experienced it myself. It's easy to get caught up in what others are doing and think, *I'll take that and make it my own.* However, if it's not aligned with your vision, unique strengths, and authentic presence, it can undermine your brand.

If you were to disappear for a month, would your business continue to thrive, or would it just operate on autopilot? If the brand feels mechanical without you, it indicates that you haven't effectively scaled your presence. Instead, you have merely created a silent machine, and machines don't attract high-ticket clients; presence does.

I want to invite you to engage in some strategic reflection prompts to help you with your current strategy and scaling efforts.

- Do I still recognize myself and my brand?
- Which parts of my strategy still feel aligned?
- What did I create because it resonated with me, and what did I build simply because it was marketed to me?
- Am I leading my business, or am I hiding behind my systems?

Here's a story that illustrates reclaiming authority.

One of my clients achieved the important milestone of hitting six figures in revenue by building a strong team. Her system was flawless, and while revenue had plateaued, she was doing everything right. However, she felt disconnected, disenchanted, and deeply misaligned.

During our work together, I didn't ask her to create a new funnel. Instead, I asked, "Where are you in this brand?" She realized that she had outsourced her voice, so we decided to strip things back.

We reclaimed her tone, simplified her offers, and elevated her presence.

In just ninety days, her audience responded as if she had been reborn. Her premium clients reactivated, and she rediscovered the passion that inspired her journey. She didn't add anything new; she simply returned to her authentic messaging. She transitioned from being automated to activated, and that alone increased her conversion rates because people don't pay for polish; they pay for presence.

Systems should support your energy. The myth that structure equates to freedom can be misleading, especially if it suffocates your identity. Yes, structure is helpful, but only when it reflects your authentic self.

The idea that "sell it and forget it" brings freedom is a myth. The truth is that "sell it and feel it" brings power.

I believe that soulful systems look and feel different from the rest. Every detail, every sound, and every email should reflect your true self. Each touchpoint must be thoughtful, not templated. Automation should respect your discernment. Soulful scaling doesn't mean doing everything; instead, it means focusing on where your power matters most.

Building a scalable, soulful business starts with your voice. You assess what you have built through the lens of who you are becoming, and from there, you rebuild your offers to reflect your current expertise, develop systems that deliver without diluting your essence, and create content that converts due to its clarity. The outcome? More sales, more alignment, and more peace.

You transform from pushing to being present.

Here's how I shifted from doing it all to doing it my way and how that changed everything for me. I walked away from launching calendars I didn't create, offers that I had outgrown, and the pressure to appear every day to be taken seriously. What I retained were my voice, depth, and discernment. Now I don't scale for visibility; I scale for sustainability.

If your business is running but you feel invisible, your systems are smooth, yet sales feel stale, or your brand is growing, but your soul is shrinking, it's time to return to your essence. Your business doesn't need more scaling; it needs more of you.

Here are some challenges to declare:

1. "My business no longer runs on autopilot; it runs on alignment."
2. "I'm no longer outsourcing my essence; I'm scaling with sovereignty."

This is one of those situations that creeps up on you. Personally, I got really excited about adopting new systems and stepping into the role of a coach, especially the strategy behind it all. However, I began to notice something wasn't right. Even though I was following the checklist and doing all the right things, it still didn't feel genuine or like it truly represented me.

At times, it was exhausting because I felt like I was pushing against my natural rhythm. It felt heavy, as if I were carrying someone else's formula or approach instead of creating my own. I experienced moments of clarity, but I also faced burnout. When I hit that stage, I realized I had been checking off boxes and following someone else's plan to the detriment of my own voice.

Once I began to pivot and align more with my voice, everything changed. It felt natural and revitalizing, and I finally felt alive. I thought, *Okay, this is me.*

You might feel like you should be taking certain actions, like launching a project or hustling harder, yet even if you achieve success and hit those milestones, it can feel hollow or misaligned. As I mentioned earlier, you may feel exhausted rather than expanded; it's as if there's pressure around you instead of a feeling of possibility.

Another sign is when you find it difficult to hear your own voice. You might end up second-guessing yourself on almost everything, from your content and marketing to your branding.

This can lead to constantly seeking others' approval or falling prey to "shiny-object syndrome," where you chase after every new trend without staying true to yourself.

It's easy to get caught up in achieving outcomes instead of focusing on alignment. This checklist mentality can become a burden.

One thing that has helped me, and still does when I find myself in that place, is to pause and ask myself what I truly want. From there, it's important to reclaim your rhythm by building systems that support your energy rather than suffocating it. Additionally, trust in your presence, story, style, and soul, as these are what truly form your brand.

I want to emphasize once again: if you feel exhausted and not expanded, that's a key indicator. Conversely, if your experience feels like expansion, then you know you're in alignment. If you sense exhaustion, burnout, or emptiness, those feelings can also serve as markers to guide you.

I believe we live in a world that prioritizes instant gratification, which affects our ego and dopamine response. When we chase likes, views, or followers, it doesn't necessarily build authority or trust. Numbers measure visibility, but they don't measure vibration. You can have the followers, the likes, and the views and still not be making real money or having a real impact.

Having hundreds of thousands of followers doesn't guarantee you'll have buyers or be able to pay your bills. I would much prefer to have a thousand aligned followers and run a multi-six-figure business than to have many followers who aren't in alignment with my brand.

This situation can be misleading, and it's important for people to understand this. Rapid growth can create a false sense of success or momentum in business. It's crucial to produce content that is authentic and resonates with your audience.

If your audience isn't converting, there's likely a disconnect between your truth and what you're sharing.

Many leaders, including me, fall into the trap of thinking that if our numbers aren't climbing, we're failing. This mindset is a reflection of societal and social media pressures. I've experienced this on various platforms, including TikTok, Facebook, and Instagram. My growth plateaued when I stopped using growth hacks and tips. However, once I became clearer about who I was speaking to and aligned my message, my business began to grow once again.

My coach at the time had around five thousand followers and was making between $40,000 and $60,000 a month. However, many people wouldn't have known that because she was so clear in her messaging and knew exactly who she was speaking to. This allowed her to attract a specific audience.

As I said before: "If you talk to everyone, you talk to no one." I repeat this often because people tend to get caught up in the follower count, believing that having more followers directly correlates to making more money or being more successful.

What's interesting is that the algorithms are always changing. However, I do know that many social media platforms encourage you to clarify who you're connecting with and to build a community around that. The more specific you are in your messaging and niche, the better the algorithm can categorize your content and connect you with people who are more aligned with your brand, leading to higher conversion rates.

I still can't believe that she is making that much money with just a few thousand followers. However, she's since grown her following by building a reputation around client success, and she has been doing this for a couple of years. Now her operation is still impressive because she has grown sustainably, unlike many others in this space who experienced rapid growth that left them questioning what had just happened.

I believe that quality is more important than quantity. Your audience must be aligned with your values, offers, and mission, period.

It's important to emphasize this point. Establishing a system is key to moving people from meeting you to trusting you and, ultimately, to investing in you. However, the soulful aspect for me involves building genuine connections, showing care, and finding alignment with those people.

I believe that the depth of your connections determines the depth of your success. And they are the structure that lets you scale without losing your heart so that every person still feels seen, cared for, and connected even as your business grows. It's not merely about a robotic, automated process; it's about the authenticity of relationship building. It's not a transaction.

As I've mentioned before, relationships drive your revenue. Every sale is essentially a relationship decision. People don't invest thousands due to a perfectly timed email; they invest because they trust you, feel safe with you, and resonate with you. If you ignore this relational aspect, you may find yourself constantly chasing sales.

I have focused on cultivating relationships throughout my life, and as a result, sales come organically and naturally. For me, the concept of a soulful system revolves around attracting aligned leads through authentic content that reflects my truth. Instead of relying on cold leads, this approach fosters connections through emails, direct messages, and the conversations I engage in.

The nurturing aspect involves maintaining these connections through those communications. When it comes to conversion, your offer should feel like a natural extension of the relationship rather than a hard sell. It's important that clients feel guided and seen throughout the process, as it encourages them to stay, renew their commitments, and refer others. This creates an organic flow in your business, which is what I consider the essence of a soulful system.

I believe that leaders need to shift their mindset from the traditional approach of prioritizing funnels over people. Instead, we should focus on building relationships first, allowing systems to amplify those relationships second. This is the key to scaling a business with loyalty rather than just volume.

Chapter Summary: Key Takeaways

- Scaling can start to feel like shrinking when a business grows in structure but loses **intimacy, meaning, and emotional connection**.
- Many women scale the "right" way by building funnels, hiring teams, and automating offers, yet end up feeling **absent inside their own business**, as if it has become a machine.
- The hidden cost of delegation is **disconnection**. When you outsource your voice without aligned support, your marketing, content, and launches can feel polished but **lifeless**.
- Scaling stalls not because of effort, but because of **process-driven burnout**. Systems may run smoothly, but without your unique energy, the brand loses resonance.
- **Growth without embodiment is an illusion**. Metrics can look strong while revenue stays stagnant and reach stays flat because emotional connection has been replaced by automation.
- The biggest revenue leaps come from **alignment and presence**, not from more automations. Scaling should **amplify your voice**, not replace it.

- Presence-led scaling means **systems serve power**. A leader-led business adapts strategy to the leader's energy, while a template-led business buries identity under rigid formulas.
- Soulful systems prioritize **relationships over transactions**. People invest because they trust you, feel safe with you, and resonate with you, not because the email sequence is perfect.
- Sustainable scaling comes from building structures that protect your essence. When you stop outsourcing your identity and scale with **sovereignty, discernment, and connection**, your business gains more sales, more peace, and more staying power.

CHAPTER 9

THE MASS SUCCESS

What does mass success look like? I believe it involves being grounded in your faith and aligning your goals with your heart. That helps you build a thriving and aligned business, one where you meet your financial goals, grow your audience, and hear the applause.

However, despite these accomplishments, you may still feel a little off.

On the outside, it seems as if everything is going well. People see you as the strong one, the example of someone who has made it. But on the inside, there can be a sense of disconnection and hollowness.

The invisible pressure of being perceived as strong means you smile in your photos, share your wins, and play the part. However, behind closed doors, you may struggle with self-doubt, feeling exhausted and unsure of how to articulate it. There's a quiet desire for change, but you continue to follow the successful playbook because it works and it's what people expect.

I've experienced this myself; there was a time when my achievements were applauded, but I secretly wondered if they were even mine anymore. On stage, I appeared confident, but behind the scenes, I felt suffocated and misaligned. Even though my success looked polished, it felt more like a cage.

This was evident during my network marketing experiences. I was doing all the right things, showing up, receiving applause on stages, and feeling successful, but inside, I felt a disconnect between who I was and who I was becoming. What the world saw was me quietly wrestling with my true feelings.

This leads to why people stay in a mask, which I describe as a psychological grip. You might ask yourself, *If I change, will I lose the trust I've built? Will people still follow me if I pivot? Am I ungrateful for everything I prayed for?* This is why success can feel sticky: one's identity becomes tied to it.

Outdated success can become a prison, and I think this hidden aspect is significant. It reflects the conflict between your brand's image and the voice that wants to expand and be heard. Perhaps you've achieved recognition for results you no longer wish to deliver, whether in your offerings or content. You may also fear outgrowing your platform.

Staying in alignment means being willing to outgrow applause. Here's the truth: alignment requires the courage to acknowledge that a previous version of yourself served its purpose but is no longer who you are. This acceptance is perfectly okay.

One of the frameworks I teach is called "Unmasking with Grace."

I have also developed a model known as the Aligned Audience Message Quadrant. The top-left side of this quadrant represents "Performing," where you are at peak performance but feel little fulfillment. The top right represents "Presence," indicating aligned energy and true authority in your messaging. The bottom left reflects "Pretending," where you are masking, burning out, and feeling disconnected. Finally, the bottom right signifies "Power," representing integrated and authentic leadership. By examining these quadrants, you can gauge your current state based on how you feel and how aligned you are with your message.

Unmasking yourself doesn't mean destroying your former identity; instead, it is about reintegration. It involves bringing forth new wisdom, embracing your truest voice, leveraging your unique experiences, and showcasing your next level of power in how you present yourself.

I think about my client Maggie a lot when I talk about identity. She was known as the go-to for content creation in her niche. Online, everything looked polished and put together, but when we started working together, I asked her a series of questions that stopped her in her tracks:

- "What are you known for that you've actually outgrown?"
- "What are you scared to say out loud?"
- "What would you launch if you weren't protecting your past image?"
- "What version of you are you still clinging to that no longer fits?"

She got quiet and said, "I don't even want to do what people know me as and what kind of content I have been putting out there." She realized she wasn't lacking strategy; she was hiding behind a version of herself that no longer reflected her skills, passion, and heart.

Maggie had been afraid to pivot because people loved the old her. But the truth was…she didn't.

Once she gave herself permission to stop protecting that old identity, everything shifted for her.

Her content became more honest and aligned, and her voice came alive. Her business started growing again, not because she did more, but because she aligned with who she was actually becoming. Her reinvention has made her more magnetic. She doesn't lose time; instead, she attracts higher-level clients who have been waiting for her true self to emerge.

Now I want to discuss the emotional courage it takes to evolve publicly. For many, this can be incredibly challenging. People often worry about what others think, fear failure, or hesitate to show their true selves due to potential judgment.

It takes courage to embrace this new reinvention and openly proclaim, "I am no longer hiding the person I once was." Creating content around this journey often involves admitting that you have been living an inauthentic, smaller version of yourself.

Now you are ready to step into your next version, unmasked and unapologetic. It's important to declare that you are not starting over; instead, you are leveling up in your expression and aligning with your truth.

Here's how reinvention affects you:

- It can change the tone of your content and marketing, shifting it from being overly polished to powerfully authentic.
- Your offerings will evolve to reflect your true zone of genius and who you really are.
- Your leadership voice will deepen, becoming more confident and resonant.
- You may find a sense of internal peace that feels more like home again.

Reinvention can be magnetic and align you with your authentic self, rather than you living a brand or voice that doesn't truly reflect who you are.

It's important to understand that reinvention doesn't erase your past; it crowns it. Everything you have built becomes the foundation for what is next for you.

Closing Charge

If you have been wearing a mask of success, hear this loud and clear: you don't owe anyone a smaller version of yourself. Your next level will come not from maintaining an image but from embodying your true self.

I have a few challenge prompts for you:

- I am no longer willing to be known for _________.
- I am ready to reintroduce a version of me that _________.
- I don't need validation for who I was; I need a vision for who I'm becoming.

This is something I am currently experiencing as I shed an identity I've held for eight years in an unhappy relationship. Daily, I receive texts or DMs saying, *"You look different. You're glowing!"* It's almost as if they think I'm pregnant! The messages I'm receiving are filled with positivity; people are happy for me rather than offering sympathy for what I'm going through.

I truly feel an energetic connection with them in a positive way. I can share more about that, but it really comes down to aligning my personal life with my business.

By showing up authentically and being true to my journey and who I'm becoming, I've been able to form deeper connections and relationships with people through DMs and conversations, even when I'm not directly trying to sell them a program or product. Remember, relationships are your revenue.

You can choose to follow certain systems or what you think is right, rather than truly engaging with what's happening in your life. Unmasking the truth about my relationship has been important for me, not in a negative way, but in a way that feels good and aligns with my authenticity.

I'm not going into detail, but I'm sharing parts of my story where I feel called by God to make decisions that will help me become a better person, a better mom, a better spouse, and a better business owner. This unmasking process this summer has brought about a significant shift for me.

For a long time, I kept following the "right" systems in business, in relationships, and in life, even when my soul was feeling like something was off. I felt like I was performing the version of myself that everyone expected: the strong, independent woman, the loyal partner, the one who could hold it all together even when things got really hard.

But behind the scenes, God kept nudging me, and I started to look at my life with honesty and conviction.

So I started peeling back the layers:

- What I tolerated.
- What I normalized.
- What I carried in silence.
- Who I had become to keep the peace.

That's when everything shifted. I realized that if I was going to be a better mom, a better woman, a better leader… I had to stop hiding behind strength and start honoring the truth.

Through this awareness, I decided to share parts of my story that would bring truth, conviction, authenticity, and relatability. I didn't share everything, but I shared what God put on my heart. What I discovered by doing this is that other women were watching me who were carrying their own challenges, identity shifts, and brave decisions. I wanted them to see that it's possible to walk through something painful without losing yourself… And sometimes, you actually can find yourself.

This experience was a part of my story of coming back home to myself. Choosing to let people witness parts of that journey has allowed me to stand in my purpose with more clarity, power, and faith than ever before.

As I've said, I've seen an increase in my stories and DMs. People appreciate this authenticity because, at times, having a large following or audience can make it seem like it's all just social media and not real life. Some might think I'm just trying to push a sale or get them involved in my business.

However, as I've embraced unmasking my relationship and this new phase of my life, it has allowed me to connect with more people, especially women who have had similar experiences. I receive long messages from women who say, *"Oh, my gosh! Me, too,"* which marks the beginning of meaningful connections.

It's essential for every business owner to remember that this type of authenticity is what truly builds a brand and a business. When you are genuine, referrals come naturally, and followers are more likely to stay engaged. They ask you, *"What are you doing now? Are you okay?"* It's almost as if they're checking in on you.

Recently, I had an "aha" moment: I realized I need to share more than just my systems and methods. It's about blending my professional and personal sides and showcasing more of my true self to unleash my realness and rawness.

Also, I believe that putting yourself out there and being real doesn't mean being exposed. Being authentic doesn't mean being unfiltered, and being a leader doesn't mean turning your wounds into content before they've healed.

Being authentic doesn't mean telling everything; it means telling the truth at the right time and for the right reasons.

I believe in being truthful about who you are without creating an image or brand that seeks approval or recognition.

It's not about ego or selfishness; it's about genuinely connecting with your audience.

My goal is to improve and step into the next version of myself. While I'm not going into all the intricate details, I recognize that there's a fine line to walk. If you share too much, you risk slipping into a victim mentality rather than celebrating your victories.

It's about transforming tribulations into triumphs. Instead of portraying life's messes, I aim to turn those experiences into a positive message that resonates with others, avoiding the impression that I'm seeking applause or approval.

I'm afraid of what people think and the judgment that comes with it. My identity often feels tied to some type of achievement. It makes me wonder, *Who am I without these accomplishments? Will it still matter if I let them go?* Letting go feels like losing a part of myself. Sometimes, wearing a mask feels safer and more comfortable.

I recognize that sitting with these feelings can feel safer as well. In network marketing, I noticed that as I rose higher, I felt there were fewer places where I could fall apart.

As I mentioned earlier, there's pressure to be the strong one, and I often feel like I'm not allowed to doubt myself. I wonder if my desires can change. People see me in a certain way, which makes me feel like I have to maintain that image. Sometimes, it seems easier to wear that mask than to risk being misunderstood.

I believe there's a lack of safe space for vulnerability in these situations. We also often convince ourselves that we should feel grateful. Even when we may not express it enough, we want to appreciate what we have. However, carrying the guilt of wanting more or feeling the need to do more can be overwhelming. For a long time, I felt that wanting more wasn't an option.

I hope that makes sense. I would say that people stay in this position not because they are weak, but because they are strong; they have learned to hold everything together, no matter the cost.

The mask they wear is evidence of their resilience, but it also becomes a barrier to their freedom.

Chapter Summary: Key Takeaways

- Mass success is not just financial growth or public applause. True success requires **alignment between faith, heart, identity, and purpose**, even when everything looks "right" on the outside.
- Many high-achieving women experience **internal disconnection beneath visible success**. They are celebrated publicly while privately feeling hollow, misaligned, or unsure if their achievements still belong to them.
- The pressure to remain "the strong one" creates a **mask of success**, where wins are shared and doubts are hidden, making evolution feel risky and lonely.
- Outdated success can become a **psychological prison** when identity becomes tied to a version of yourself you have already outgrown, even if that version is admired by others.
- Alignment requires the courage to **outgrow applause**. Honoring who you are becoming means accepting that a past version served its purpose and no longer defines you.
- Reinvention is not destruction. **Unmasking with grace** is about reintegration, bringing forward new wisdom,

deeper truth, and expanded leadership without erasing the past.

- Public evolution takes emotional courage. Declaring "I am no longer hiding" can feel vulnerable, but it often leads to **greater resonance, authority, and inner peace**.
- When a woman stops protecting her old identity, her content, offers, and leadership voice **come alive**, attracting higher-level clients who were waiting for her true expression.
- Authenticity builds relationships, and **relationships drive revenue**. When you show up from truth rather than performance, deeper connections naturally form.
- The mask of success is proof of strength, not weakness. But freedom comes when strength is no longer used to hide. **True power emerges when identity, faith, and expression are aligned**, allowing both business and life to expand with integrity.

CHAPTER 10

THE REAL REASONS OFFERS AREN'T CONVERTING

Many of my clients struggle to recognize their worth based on their experiences. Take my client Brianna. She was on the verge of losing her large business but believed that it wasn't a failure; it was just not the right fit for her. Similarly, my clients Maggie and Lakeisha participated in a digital program that seemed promising at first, but it turned out to be misaligned with their goals. They had to refocus and gain clarity around their positioning and business direction.

On my end, I successfully launched my first mastermind and retreat, which allowed me to build relationships and connect deeply with my clients. Remember, your relationships generate your revenue. Within just fifteen days, strangers turned into clients and, ultimately, friends. I vividly recall my first week earning $33,000, which was a huge accomplishment for me.

I hosted an in-person retreat and gathered women to express their desires, identities, visions, missions, and the legacies they wanted to leave, all based on their unique skills, expertise, and life experiences.

The False Diagnosis

There are moments when your engagement dips, your sales calls don't go well, and your launches fall short of expectations. During these times, your confidence can wane, which impacts how you present yourself and your offer.

This can lead to panic and result in a low conversion rate because energy is transferable; it's all about frequency. How you show up affects how others perceive you and what you project into the world. Your connection with clients and ability to portray yourself as an authority often falter, causing anxiety and self-doubt.

The spiral usually begins with questioning myself: *Is my price too high? Do I need to change my niche? Is the market too saturated? Should I develop a better sales funnel?* I vividly recall the same discussions happening in network marketing. When there is a sudden influx of people, likes, engagement, and sales, and then that momentum dips for various reasons, people start to question everything, including the price, niche, and tactics. In reality, much of this is tied to energy and how authentically they are showing up for their audience and themselves.

I've seen so many women spiral into a frenzy, changing their copy, adjusting prices, rebranding frequently, and chasing the latest shiny objects. They believe they can resolve their struggles by addressing surface-level issues like a broken funnel, an obscure algorithm, or an uninterested audience. The truth lies in pulling back the layers. It's not about tactical changes; it's about energy and authenticity.

I believe many of them become careful with their voices instead of clear and confident. I once had a client whose messaging we refined together. We clarified her offer, yet instead of following the aligned path we established, she veered in the opposite direction. She began to create a brand that wasn't truly hers, attempting superficial fixes rather than focusing on her core truth. Influenced by others around her, she started implementing tactical changes that aligned with trends instead of her authentic self. Eventually, she returned to me, seeking guidance, realizing that she had strayed from her initial vision.

The real truth isn't just about what you're selling; it's about who your brand is when you make the sale. Watered-down messaging often affects powerful women. This is how they unintentionally dim their brilliance.

Sometimes, a woman may fear being too assertive, so she softens her message. Being multi-gifted can lead her to combine everything into one offer, resulting in a muddled and confusing message. She might be advised to niche down, which can cause her to cut away parts of her brilliance just to appear marketable. I see this often in this space, constantly hearing "niche down, niche down." In reality, many talents and gifts can enhance marketing and offers, but they are often neglected due to this advice.

An energetic drop occurs when your voice shifts from being clear to overly cautious. When this happens, your audience can no longer connect with you. As discussed in previous chapters, your audience's emotional response matters. When your offer starts to sound like everyone else's, even if your work is truly life-changing, you risk that energetic drop.

The framework I teach is clarity that converts.

Think of it this way: conversion equals clarity multiplied by confidence. If either of these elements is missing, your results will plateau. You need both clarity and confidence to drive conversion.

Conversion isn't about coercing people or running flashy sales campaigns; it's about capturing attention through crystal-clear clarity. Your message should cut through the noise, command attention, and establish your authority.

Ask yourself:

- What is my brand actually conveying?
- What do I assume people know about my offer that I haven't communicated clearly?
- Where might I be hiding behind vague language or industry jargon?
- Does my offer feel bold or just nice?
- Would I buy this if I saw it from someone else?

One of my clients had a brilliant offer, complete with testimonials, results, and heart, but she kept changing her prices, funnel, and ads because nothing was converting. When we cut through the noise, we discovered the core issue: her messaging was vague, cautious, and safe. I remember it vividly; she often labeled her audience as "broke people." I had to shift her mindset and point out that there are people in her audience who aren't broke.

Shifting how she viewed herself transformed how her audience engaged with her, leading them to want to work with her through her webinars and the new course she created. This newfound clarity gave her the confidence that her approach was effective.

Once she showed up with more clarity, her numbers improved. Her conversion rates increased, her confidence grew, and she began making sales in a shorter time. It wasn't a matter of waiting months for results; enrolling new clients became significantly easier.

This success didn't stem from changing her offer but from embracing her authority when presenting it. Ultimately, it comes down to the messaging and how it resonates with your ideal million-dollar client. This is the new standard for conversion.

There is a significant difference between merely saying, "Here's what I offer," and clearly articulating, "Here's what happens when you work with me." Your brand can either whisper or roar, and your offer can either blend in or break patterns.

Women who sell effortlessly are often the ones with high-ticket offers, despite not necessarily being the cheapest option available. They are polished, clear, and fully embody their messages, which is palpable to their audience.

Stop wondering if the market is saturated. Addressing this myth directly is powerful. The market isn't oversaturated; it's your message that may be too safe. There is always room for boldness and for women who lead with authority and truth.

Here's how you can reframe that perspective. Reframe "converting" as a call to rise rather than a cue to retreat. Most of your sales challenges can be resolved not by increasing ad spend but by raising your standards.

Your audience doesn't need another safe offer. They need your clear, unapologetic voice. They want to harness your authority and see the version of you that refuses to shrink.

If I could say anything to my audience without fear, I would say, "You don't need a new system or another blueprint. What you truly need is to believe in yourself the way I already believe in you. Stop waiting for the perfect plan. Your life is already urging you to take action."

The unique result I create, one that no one else can replicate, is helping women step out of the masks they've been wearing, reconnect with their true voices, and build businesses that actually feel like home. These businesses should not only be profitable but also peaceful; not just visible, but aligned.

I refuse to dumb down my brand to make it more digestible. I'm here to roar with clarity, to take up space unapologetically, and to inspire the women who are ready to stop playing small and rise.

Many women who are masking or conforming to what most people do often hide their true selves behind a façade. When I read someone's content, I can usually tell if it's scripted. It's important to help them embrace their truth and guide them back to what they genuinely believe. Using journal prompts can help them realign with their authentic selves and generate content that is bold, authentic, and presents a version of them that is done playing small or hiding. The real power lies in the content that they were originally afraid to say out loud.

Reframing is crucial. If people feel hesitant about what to say or what content to share, I encourage them to ask themselves: *What's the worst that could happen?* Practicing is key; it's essential to create content that feels genuine. If their content feels flat or doesn't represent an unapologetic version of themselves, I advise them not to post it.

Additionally, anchoring in embodiment is important. It's not just about the words you use; it's also about your tone, presence, and energy. Recently, I've been radiating a different energy that conveys happiness, and people are drawn to my journey. I remind them that if they believe in themselves, others will feel it, too.

This principle applies not just to sales but to everything else we do. Your confidence sells as much as your clarity does.

Focus on reframing your mindset. If you believe *It didn't work, so I must have failed,* try thinking, *It didn't work yet*. The shift that is required to reframe is to realize that you may be outgrowing an old version of your messaging, energy, and identity. Ask yourself, *What part of me is being asked to evolve so my audience feels me again?* This is not failing; it is a call to **rise** and **evolve**.

Just a simple word change can shift your thoughts from negative to positive. For example, instead of thinking, *Maybe I should lower my prices, niche down, or change my offer*, consider it an opportunity to sharpen your clarity without abandoning your calling.

Often, you hear people say things like, "The market must be too saturated." Instead of that, you could think, *If it didn't land, I'm not broken. I'm just invited to show up even bolder and be okay with pivoting or changing my messaging a bit.*

Whenever doubts, fears, or feelings of shrinking or hiding arise, get curious. Refine your voice and raise your standards instead of lowering your prices. I actually heard this just yesterday during a call with a fitness coach. He mentioned that the market is oversaturated and that he was lowering his prices. I encouraged him to reconsider that perspective.

I don't think that oversaturation is the real issue. Instead, it's about being bolder and getting clearer on who you serve and how you can help, especially during times when people aren't spending as much as they were six, nine, or twelve months ago.

Chapter Summary: Key Takeaways

- Many women misdiagnose stalled sales or low engagement as tactical problems when the real issue is often **energy, clarity, and authenticity**, not funnels, pricing, or algorithms.
- When confidence dips, women tend to spiral into surface-level fixes like rebranding, lowering prices, or chasing trends. This reaction usually **dims their authority instead of restoring it**.
- Watered-down messaging happens when powerful women become cautious instead of clear. **Softening**

your voice to feel safer creates an energetic drop that your audience immediately feels.

- Conversion is driven by **clarity multiplied by confidence**. If either one is missing, the results plateau, regardless of how good the offer actually is.
- Being multi-gifted is not a weakness. Cutting away parts of your brilliance to "niche down" often creates **confusion instead of connection** when done without discernment.
- The difference between effortless sellers and struggling ones is not price or popularity. It is **embodied authority**, clear messaging, and the courage to speak boldly rather than blend in.
- When something doesn't convert, it is rarely a failure. It is an invitation to **refine your voice, raise your standards, and evolve your identity**, not abandon your calling.

CONCLUSION

YOU'RE NOT BEHIND, JUST BEING POSITIONED

This is the pause before the rise. If you've made it this far, let me assure you: you're not starting over. You're shedding what no longer fits.

You're not broken; you're being rebuilt with precision. This isn't failure; it's evolution. Content fatigue was never about laziness. You never hated marketing; you hated filtering your voice.

You never lacked discipline; you lacked alignment. You weren't inconsistent; you were incomplete. But now you know better.

You no longer need to perform; you get to be seen. You get to speak, and you get to lead. You're not leading from a script anymore; you're leading from your authentic self.

You're not behind, just being positioned. This is your permission slip to release guilt, forgive the detour, and reframe the delay. You didn't just shift strategies; you reclaimed your mission.

You're no longer editing your messaging; you're embodying your true identity.

Before, you felt burned out, boxed in, and underwhelmed. Now you're clear, bold, magnetic, and positioned to lead from the front.

Take a moment for self-reflection. Declare this with me: "I'm not just pivoting; I'm evolving. My voice is not too much; it's powerful. From this day forward, I give myself permission to speak my truth."

These aren't just statements; they are declarations. This is the moment you draw a line in the sand.

This book wasn't just a strategy. It was permission. It was a mirror. It was a fire starter.

If you're done shrinking your brilliance into boxes that no longer fit, if you're ready to build a business that matches your frequency, not just your resume, then…

Next, we will focus on my mastermind program. Together, we will rebuild your brand from the inside out, helping you reconnect with your divine purpose. We will rise with a strategy that incorporates soul and structure, allowing you not only to increase your income but also your impact.

This is for the woman who has already built her foundation but now realizes she is called to lead. Remember, we're just getting started.

Follow me on Instagram @keisha_leilani and explore the movement at keishaleilani.com.

Let's embark on this journey together.

THANK YOU FOR READING MY BOOK!

Thank you for choosing this book and
for being willing to sit with what it stirred inside you.
I'd love to gift you a few free bonuses, no strings attached!

Scan the QR code:

If this book resonated with you, I'd be honored
if you shared your experience by leaving a review on Amazon.
Your words help this message reach the women who are
quietly standing at the edge of their own becoming.
Thank you for being here.

www.ingramcontent.com/pod-product-compliance
Lightning Source LLC
LaVergne TN
LVHW090527110826
845146LV00003B/1012